THE "NIGHTINGALE" SCANDAL

By Stanley Thomas

WITH DRAWINGS BY JOHN DYKE

2001
Lazarus Press
Bideford

First published 1959

This edition 2001
Published by Myrtle Ternstrom
Cheltenham GL53 9DE

Isbn 0 9523062 3 9

THE
"NIGHTINGALE"
SCANDAL

Stanley Thomas

Typeset, Printed & Bound by
Lazarus Press
Unit 7 Caddsdown Business Park
Bideford
Devon EX39 3DX

FOREWORD

This intriguing and well-researched book
was first published by Stanley Thomas in 1959,
and has now become a rarity
as it has been out of print since then.

I am most grateful to Mrs Kathleen Uren, of Barnstaple,
who has kindly given her permission
for her late brother's work to be reprinted.

I am also indebted to my good friend, John Dyke,
who has allowed the reproduction of his
original illustrations.

The original text is printed unaltered,
but some short notes are added
from my own research into the history of Lundy.

Myrtle Ternstrom, 2001

CONTENTS

INTRODUCTION

In the early part of the eighteenth century a wealthy aristocracy lorded the land. Rich and all-powerful they controlled the government and the laws of England. Men such as the Duke of Newcastle, who owned property in twelve counties and whose income was some forty thousand pounds a year, became a class apart and built themselves stately rural palaces furnished with works of art culled from every corner of the earth. Under their princely patronage the fine arts flourished and the English craftsman developed his skill to the point of perfection. But behind its facade, as elegant and spacious as the great houses of the period, with their gardens and rolling parklands, laid out by fashionable landscape gardeners, life for the common people was stark and brutal. Abject poverty and disease corroded the spirit of England. The prints of Hogarth point the despair and the starved lean faces of his time. This was the period of "The Beggars' Opera" – an age of vice and corruption.

The rich protected their property by savage laws. For stealing a handkerchief, as long as it was taken privily from the person, a young child could be hanged by the neck until dead; for petty theft the punishment was transportation and public hangings became a frequent occurrence.

In contrast to the elegant houses of the rich the poor lived in hovels of one or two rooms. In the larger cities houses and cellars were overcrowded - ten people to a room was not uncommon. Under such conditions disease was rife and spread unchecked; epidemics of smallpox, cholera, and typhoid made death common-place.

Seeking some escape from their despair, from disease and the ever-present shadow of death the people found an outlet in drink, in gambling, and in acts of violence and crime. Some found relief from their taut feelings by listening to the emotional preaching of John Wesley. Their sobbing, weeping, and laughter provided an hysterical accompaniment to his services. Nothing stirred them so deeply as when he preached of death and hell and the toughest members of his congregation had convulsions and fits of hysteria.

In the years of lean harvests the lot of the common people became unbearable. Driven by hunger into food riots, looting and burning, they were ruthlessly suppressed by the militia and punished by hangings and mass transportations. With bitterness and much justification they felt that there was, indeed, one law for the rich and another for the poor.

The middle of the century, however, saw a challenge to the autocratic power of the land-owning aristocracy. A great increase in the wealth and commerce of England brought fortunes to the merchant princes who traded with Europe, with the colonies of America, with India, and the Far East. Their growing wealth gained them political influence and, like the great landowners, they bought estates and built themselves fine houses. They acquired, too, the social prestige which went with the ownership of land and this enabled them to marry their sons and daughters into the aristocracy.

*   *   *   *   *   *   *   *   *   *

The pages that follow give an account of the career of a merchant of these times; a man no better and, perhaps, no worse than his contemporaries, who traded from a small port in Devonshire, but whose name was to become known throughout the land.

CHAPTER I

THE MERCHANT ADVENTURER

Appledore, in North Devon, a small fishing village, its narrow crooked streets broken by slipways giving sudden glimpses of the sea, lies at the spot where the two rivers, Taw and Torridge, meet and flow together over the bar out into the Atlantic. Not far away are the two rival towns of Barnstaple and Bideford. Barnstaple, at the head of the Taw estuary, was the principal town of North Devon since early Saxon times, proudly claiming itself to be one of the oldest boroughs in the Kingdom. For centuries it had been a busy, thriving port, but gradually its harbour silted up and by the eighteenth century most of its foreign trade was lost to Bideford. Until Elizabethan times, Bideford was regarded as a town of very little consequence, but grew rapidly from the time that Sir Richard Grenville colonised Virginia and Carolina. Fostered by Grenville this small town on the Torridge built up a considerable trade with the colonies which continued for over two hundred years, ending only when the American colonies gained their independence. By the eighteenth century the flourishing trade of Bideford was a serious threat to the prosperity of the merchants of Barnstaple.

Daniel Defoe writing in 1724 reported that "These two rival towns are really very considerable, both of them have a large share in the trade to Ireland and in the herring fishery, and in the trade to the British colonies in America; if Biddiford cures more fish, Barnstaple imports more wine and other merchandises; they are both established ports for landing wool from Ireland. If Biddiford has a greater number of merchants, Barnstaple has a greater commerce within land, by its great market for Irish wool and yarn etc., with the serge makers of Tiverton and Excester who come up hither to buy. So that in a word, Barnstaple, though it has lost ground to Biddiford, yet, take it in all its trade completely is full as considerable to Bideford; only that perhaps it was formerly superior to it, and the other has risen up to be a match to it."

At this time Squire John Benson, a respected merchant of Bideford, and his family lived at Knapp House, built on the hill rising above Appledore and overlooking the estuary of the two rivers. He had three sons, John, Peter and Thomas, and a daughter Catherine. In 1707,

Thomas Benson, the youngest of Squire John's sons, was born. Nothing remarkable is recorded of him as a young man. He married his cousin, Frances Melhuish, at Taunton in 1737, who bore him a family of two sons, Peter and John, and a daughter Grace. His eldest brother, John, following the family tradition became a merchant and lived at Parkham, which lies half-way between Bideford and Clovelly. John died in 1738. Squire Benson died the following year and Peter inherited the family estates and business. Peter, the cautious member of the family, never married and in a few years acquired considerable property of his own. On his death in 1743 all this, apart from certain properties left on trust for his nieces and nephews, together with the family estates, business and home at Knapp House was left to Thomas. This inheritance was said to be worth £40,000, though this estimate was probably an exaggeration. At any rate he was comfortably off and could well have led the pleasant life of a country squire, but this did not satisfy his restless and ambitious nature.

His brother Peter, cautious and prudent, had carried on the family business since the death of their father, trading with France and Portugal and the colonies of America. In 1739, four years before his death, war broke out between England and Spain. The causes of the war had been gathering force for some time. For many years the English merchants had resented the right of search by the Spanish "Guarda-costas" who were often little better than licensed pirates and had confiscated English cargoes and sometimes seized the ships themselves on the slightest of pretexts. The government of Sir Robert Walpole was anxious to avoid war with Spain but were forced by the merchants, who saw that their expanding trade with the colonies was at stake, into the declaration of war with Spain.

The war was mainly a war at sea and brought increasing dangers to English merchant shipping. Peter Benson in his will prudently advised his brother Thomas to sell his vessels because of the growing hazard of the times, but Thomas was of a very different temperament from his brother and such advice was not likely to appeal to his bold and enterprising nature.

This was the period of the great merchant princes, when the West country merchants of Bristol were amassing vast fortunes from the tobacco trade with Virginia and from the even more profitable slave trade. From his boyhood, Thomas Benson had watched the ships sailing across the bar from Barnstaple and Bideford to France, Spain and Portugal, or across the Atlantic to the American colonies; and as a boy had spent many hours listening to sailors' tales on Appledore Quay. The call was irresistible; the hazards of the times brought an added zest. Here he found the true outlet for his tremendous ability, his energy and his drive. He became the very life-blood of the commerce of the ports of Appledore and Bideford trading with Portugal, importing tobacco and exporting the locally made woollen goods to the colonies of Maryland and Virginia and sending a fleet of between forty and fifty fishing vessels every year to the Newfoundland fisheries. In addition to all this he manufactured rope and carried on a profitable business as a coal merchant.

The Tobacco trade of Bideford was very considerable indeed. For half a century, from 1700 until 1750, Bideford merchants imported in their own ships more tobacco than any other port in England with the exception of London. At the peak of this period nearly a million tons of tobacco were imported every year.

Every year, too, the fishing fleet, some fifty sail of ships set out from Bideford for the Newfoundland Fisheries. Most of the inhabitants of Bideford and Appledore were employed in storing up the fleet with food, including hard biscuits and drinking water. The grand banks swarmed with codfish in such vast dense shoals that they sometimes stopped the progress of the vessels. Here the fleet remained for several months, fishing by line for long, cold weary hours, their clothing soaked, and having no means of drying themselves the crews remained permanently wet. Frequently a thick fog would cover the ocean and there was rarely a season when one of the vessels was not wrecked through drifting in the fog on to the coast of Labrador or Iceland.

The fish were cured in brine and were re-exported to the Mediterranean, to Holland and, before war broke out, to France and Spain.

In March 1744 France entered the war as an ally of Spain. The trade of the English merchants became even more hazardous. Thomas Benson fitted out one of his vessels, the *Benson Galley*, as a man of war and fought the French and Spanish as a privateer. One can imagine the *Benson Galley* sailing over the bar to raid Spanish and French shipping in the same spirit as Sir Richard Grenville had set out with five small ships to meet the threat of the Spanish Armada some two hundred years earlier, and as two hundred years later a handful of M.T.B.'s set out from the same small port to make a daring attack on the German submarine base at St. Nazaire.

Privateers, like the Spanish "Guard costas," officially licensed pirates, were private men of war fitted out by merchants or adventurers who received letters of marque authorising them to plunder the King's enemies. The cost of these ships was borne out of the plunder of which the Crown received a proportion. The crew received no wages but each man was given a share of the loot. At this time there were some 99 English Privateers and a similar number were fitted out by the American colonies. The *Benson Galley*, the only privateer to operate from North Devon, carried twenty guns and a crew of 180. One of the crew was a young tough in his 'teens, James Bather, who had been at sea since he was eleven years old and was later to play a fateful part in the career of Thomas Benson.

The *Benson Galley* was commanded by Captain Richard Vernan, a man highly regarded for his bravery and fighting qualities. In January of the year, when in command of one of Benson's trading vessels, the *Britannia,* he had been engaged by a Spanish privateer of some ten six-pounder guns about eighty leagues west of Cape Clear. After an hour's engagement the Privateer put a boarding party on the *Britannia* and engaged her crew at close quarters. Within half an hour the members of the boarding party were either dead or taken prisoner, and when the Captain of the Privateer realised what had happened to his men he sent a second party aboard the *Britannia*, who shared the same fate as the others. Captain Vernan then bore down on the Spanish privateer in an attempt to capture her but she made off, and the *Britannia* "being a foul bottom ship" was soon out-run. Out of a total crew of one hundred men the Spaniards lost in this encounter some 84 either killed, or taken prisoner and brought back to Barnstaple. Not one man of the *Britannia's* crew was lost or even, indeed, wounded.

This exploit thrilled the people of North Devon and brought Captain Vernan national fame.

Against the French the *Benson Galley* fought a brief, glorious but unprofitable war. On July 11th, 1744, she surprised and took two French vessels, the *St. William* of Honfleur and the *Mary and Anne* of Granville, both laden with fish, and carried them into St. John's harbour. In September she captured a richer prize, taking a further seven French fishing vessels off the Newfoundland fishing banks. The value of these prizes was ten thousand pounds a vessel. A month later, however, when escorting four of Benson's merchant vessels *Britannia, Mont, Prosperous* and *Vine* bound from Newfoundland to Lisbon, she had the misfortune to encounter, some fifty leagues S.S.W. from Cape Finisterre, two French men-of-war, of forty-four guns and three hundred men each. Resistance was useless against such overwhelming odds even for so valiant a fighter as Captain Vernan. The *Benson Galley* and the other vessels were seized as prize by the French.

Another of Benson's captains, Alexander Ley, master of the *Newkey*, was to distinguish himself in an encounter with the French later that year. The Gentleman's Magazine of November 1744 reports the incident as follows:– "This evening arrived in this port (Barnstaple) the *Pierre and Marie*, a French Privateer of 35 tons, 47 men, six carriage guns and four swivel guns Capt. John Lacoast, belonging to Morlaix, who on the 19th instant met in latitude 51.15 about 15 leagues to the westward of Cape Clear, the *Newkey* of this port, Alexander Ley, master, 13 guns, 13 men, 71 passengers (Irishmen) and 15 French prisoners: after a few shot the privateer boarded the *Newkey* with thirty men; the Irish passengers refused to fight, and stayed on deck; on which Capt. Ley and his 12 brave fellows retreated to close quarters, and fired promiscuously amongst French and Irish; some of the foremost of the French were killed and the rest retreated: They boarded a second, and the third time, with their Captain, who took the dead Irishmen and stopt the holes thro' which Capt. Ley and his people fir'd, then cut up the decks and threw down granadoes and a stinkpot, on which Capt. Ley surrender'd who had but one of his own people killed; but there were 31 Irishmen killed and 30 wounded. Capt. Ley had his shoulder-bone broke by a musket which he fir'd thro' the hole at the French captain as he was cutting the deck, and which wounded the latter in the hand, and the ball grazed his cheek. The captain of the privateer took Capt. Ley on board his ship and put him in his own bed, used the men very well, because he said, they were very brave fellows: the Irish he put in the *Newkey's* long boat, tur'd them adrift, being about 12 leagues from Ireland. There were eight French killed and ten wounded, several of the latter are like to die. On the 23rd inst., the privateer made Hartland and Lundy, which he took for the coast of France; but finding his mistake, and being very leaky, he gave up his commission to Capt. Ley and surrendered himself and people. The

French captain is now here (Barnstaple), as are the wounded, the rest are sent to Plymouth."

In September of the following year Captain Ley, now in command of the vessel *Resolution*, on a voyage from Barnstaple to Newfoundland, was himself taken by two French privateers.

Such were the fortunes of war. Despite all its hazards Benson's trade continued to flourish and he became, no doubt to the chagrin of the Barnstaple merchants, the outstanding merchant of North Devon.

His wealth, influence and unusual ability were recognised by prominent members of the Whig government, and rewarded by investing Benson with the high office of Sheriff of Devon in 1746. At the same time it was suggested to him that if he cared to offer himself as a candidate in the next parliamentary election, he would received the full support of the Whig party.

His political friends were powerful indeed. Lord Carteret, Secretary of State, and his cousin, Lord Gower, the Lord Privy Seal. Both had interests in North Devon as had their family, the Grenvilles for many years before them. Lord Gower, moreover, was one of the electors on the Register of the borough of Barnstaple. The Parliamentary representation of this borough was controlled by the Corporation and Benson's first task was to win their approval. He started his campaign early in 1745. A candidate in a previous election had presented the Corporation with their portraits painted by Hudson, which are still to be seen hanging in the Barnstaple Guildhall. Benson presented the Corporation with a magnificent silver punchbowl, one of the finest pieces of the Borough plate. This splendid gesture appears to have been well received by the Corporation, for in the election that followed, Benson, together with Henry Rolle, were duly returned as Members of Parliament.

The Election was a curious one. The sudden dissolution of Parliament in June, 1747, came unexpectedly, finding both sides unprepared and, no doubt, since it was well known that Rolle, who had represented the Borough for many years, was soon to be made a peer, it was agreed by both sides to postpone the fight till the vacancy, that would be thus created, occurred. Benson was extremely fortunate in not having to contest his seat, and his gift of a silver punch-bowl to the Corporation represented a moderate outlay compared with the expenditure of the two candidates, Mr. John Fortescue and Sir Bouchier Wrey, in the bye-election that ensued. (The Fortescues and the Wreys still play a prominent part in the life of Devon as they have done for centuries past.)

Mr. John Fortescue, supported in his candidature by the Prince of Wales, who was opposed to the leading members of the Government, opened his campaign during the General Election. Benson contributed five hundred pounds to his fighting fund. It is a curious fact that Benson, a supporter of the Government, should contribute so handsomely to a candidate representing the opposition, and may well explain why Mr. Fortescue decided not to contest the constituency until the bye-election.

For the ten days from the receipt of the Election Writ to the declaration of the Poll, Mr. Fortescue entertained all and sundry with 12 bottles of ale, five of cider, 456 bottles of wine and £25 worth of "drinks of all sorts"; the only solids of which there are mention being a salmon 10/- and "on the day he came to town" 27/- worth of eatables which were washed down with 111 bottles of wine, besides punch, beer, cider and ale. Altogether, £159 was spent in this preliminary cultivation of the constituency. Though so many potent arguments were brought to bear on the stomachs of the electorate, other methods of influencing opinions were not neglected; and the procession which is so prominent a feature of American electioneering seems to have been forestalled at Barnstaple by a "Cavalcade," whose drummers and trumpeters got a guinea and a half for their services.

The electorate only numbered 323 voters, a very mixed lot including 3 peers, one of whom was Lord Gower, and 3 destitute freemen "in ye workhouse." All except 25 of the rank and file of the electors received a bribe or "loan" as it was recorded in the account books from Mr. Fortescue, the recognised sum being twenty guineas.

At the beginning of August, Mr. Fortescue's agent wrote informing him of the canvass that had been made at the end of July, which showed him to be slightly ahead of Sir Bouchier Wrey. At the foot of his letter was, however, an ominous P.S. "Mr. Benson seems very uneasy about ye 500 1" – The astute Benson had sensed the way the wind was blowing. Perhaps he saw no reason why he should contribute to the fighting funds of a candidate opposed to the Government which he supported, and from which he might hope for several valuable contracts and future favours.

The next canvass taken at the end of September was by no means as favourable. It showed Sir Bouchier Wrey well in the lead, and though Mr. Fortescue had won over three of Sir Bouchier's supporters, this was more than balanced by losing five of his own – and the support of Thomas Benson. He was by no means the only voter in the Borough who changed his opinion; the records show that some of them did not act without good reason, and the arguments may have been as cogent in his case as theirs.

After laying out nearly £4,000 and finding his prospects of election growing less and less, Mr. Fortescue, on the advice of the Prince of Wales, withdrew from the campaign, and Sir Bouchier Wrey was duly elected unopposed in the bye-election, and no doubt re-paid Benson well for his valuable and timely support.

Benson had every reason to be pleased with the result of the election but it was only to be expected that several of his rival merchants of Barnstaple should view his success with misgiving and envy.

CHAPTER II

THE MEMBER FOR BARNSTAPLE

On Thursday, November 12th, 1747, His Majesty King George II went to the House of Peers and opened the new session of Parliament with a most gracious speech. The King's speech was entirely concerned with the war with Spain and France, and in his message to the House of Commons he desired them "to grant me such supplies, as your security and lasting welfare and the present critical and important situation of affairs, require."

The war was now in its eighth year. By the early part of 1747 the enemy had captured more than twelve hundred British ships and caused great anxiety to the merchants of this country. The declaration of war in 1739 had been an occasion for public rejoicing; bells were rung and the Prince of Wales toasted the mob from a city tavern. Almost alone Sir Robert Walpole, the head of the government, was opposed to the war. He continued in office for a further two years but his heart was no longer in it, and the vigour which had sustained him in power for more than twenty years was fast ebbing away. On his resignation in 1742 Lord Cartaret as Secretary of State virtually ruled as "sole minister." His policy of committing England to a continental war proved so expensive and unpopular with its greatly increased taxation that, although Cartaret was a great favourite with George II, the King was forced to appoint Henry Pelham as his chief minister, the First Lord of the Treasury. By 1747 Henry Pelham and his brother the Duke of Newcastle controlled the government of the country.

The Duke of Newcastle had a remarkable genius for electioneering politics, and over a period of forty years he controlled government patronage with an extraordinary zest and skill. Before his time no government had fully exploited this art, but Newcastle made certain that even the most petty official of the Customs and Excise, or in the service of the Admiralty or the Post Office used his vote in accordance with the government's instructions or else lost his job. This meant that any candidate in the seaports who received Newcastle's support was fairly sure of being elected. There were other forms of patronage too, for instance the granting of government contracts, that made it politic for ambitious Members of Parliament, especially those with commercial interests, to keep well in with the Duke.

Dr. Johnson had a poor opinion of the Whig party. "At the time of the Revolution," he said, "Whiggism was accompanied with certain principles; but latterly, as a mere party distinction under Walpole and the Pelhams, was no better than the politics of stock jobbers, and the religion of infidels."

Thomas Benson, now in his fortieth year, was sworn in with the newly elected members and took his seat as member for Barnstaple. One of the first matters that came before the new House was a bill "to prohibit insurance on ships belonging to France and the merchandise laden therein." Doubtful, as it is, whether Benson took any part in the debate on this bill, it seems extremely probable that it touched off an idea in his shrewd and lively mind which was to have a profound effect on his future career.

Benson, indeed, possessed most of the attributes necessary for a successful Parliamentary career; a wealthy and respected merchant, extremely able, a persuasive and forceful speaker, combined with a personality of great charm. More than this, he had influential friends in the Government. However much of his energy and ability he devoted to the interests of his constituency, he certainly lost no time in promoting his own interests, and within a few months of his election he obtained from the Government a valuable contract. In October of that year Benson was aware of the talk of peace in Government circles. During the year Anson and Hawke had won great naval victories for England, and the financial and economic position of France was becoming desperate. With the loss of Louisburg the French participation in the rich Newfoundland fisheries was at a standstill, and her trade was at the mercy of the victorious English fleets. England, on the other hand, had actually increased her import and export trade progressively during the war. Benson, looking for an expansion of his own trade, secured a contract for shipping convicts to the colonies of Maryland and Virginia. His powerful friends, Lord Gower and Lord Cartaret, were, no doubt, of great assistance in obtaining this through their influence with the Duke of Newcastle.

In that brutal age, prisons were chiefly used for detaining debtors and those awaiting trial or execution, and most offenders against the law were transported to the colonies. A contract with the government for their transportation assured a merchant of a continuous and profitable traffic for his vessels. When, at last, peace was signed with France, Benson was ready to push ahead with his plans to consolidate his position as the leading merchant of North Devon.

His contact with Lord Gower and Lord Cartaret, descendants of Sir Richard Grenville, enabled him to lease from them the following year, at a rental of £60 per annum, the Island of Lundy, which was part of their family estate, and had been acquired by Grenville in settlement of a debt.

Lundy, a small Island in the Bristol Channel, lies some twenty miles to the west of Appledore and within view of Benson's house at Knapp. The Island at that time was in a derelict state; the buildings in decay, the land uncultivated, and the Island over-run by rats and rabbits. In 1721, the previous tenant, Richard Scores, fell foul of the customs for smuggling, and since that time the Island had been uninhabited. At first sight its appeal to an enterprising merchant is hard to understand, as it seemed to represent a source of considerable expense rather than profit.

But Benson had clear, if original, ideas about the Island. He intended to use it as a sort of bonded warehouse for his merchandise or, as was viewed by the Customs, as a base for smuggling.

The records of the Court of Exchequer show that in May 1750 Benson, together with William Hammett, master of his vessel the *Grace*, and a certain Peter Marshall, mariner in Benson's employ, were in trouble with the Collector of Customs for Barnstaple over duty due on "British Plantation Tobacco" imported into the port of Barnstaple in the *Grace* on January 11th 1749. The duty and penalties demanded by the customs amounted to £922. Benson disputed this and the case was to drag on for nearly three years. It is a great pity that the Custom's Records for this period are not available but unfortunately they were destroyed in a fire at the London Customs House in 1814. There is reason, however, to believe that the tobacco in question was landed on Lundy. That he had other profitable uses for the Island is made clear by an account of the visit to Lundy by Benson and some guests in 1752.

The guests, who included Sir Thomas Gunson, Sheriff of Somerset, had been staying in Knapp. Benson proposed that they should visit his island domain and took his young nephew, Thomas Stafford, the son of his sister Catherine and a great favourite of his, on the expedition. The party embarked at Appledore in a vessel bound for South Wales, and were taken ashore from Lundy Roads in a small boat. As they approached the Island on that summer's day they were impressed by its air of peacefulness and tranquillity. The high cliffs on the eastern side covered with the fresh green of the young bracken, glinting and sparkling in the sunshine, where the bare granite broke through, sloped steeply down to the clearest of calm water. Curving away crescent-wise to the south-east the high cliffs taper down to small rocky islets, reaching out into the sea, and forming a semi-circular bay and a safe anchorage. Here the party landed and climbed to the top of the Island by a steep and difficult path.

It is fortunate that one of the party wrote an account of this visit which gives an authentic picture of the Island and an amusing glimpse of Benson himself. He writes: "We landed about two o'clock. Mr. Benson did not accompany us expecting letters from the Insurance Office for the vessel and cargo that was to take us there." (Benson's guests could have had no idea of the importance and significance of these letters from the Insurance Office.) "The vessel then lay off his quay with convicts bound for Virginia, and he came to us on Wednesday and staid till the Saturday following, when we returned in a brisk gale to Appledore.

"The Island at this time was in no state of improvement, the houses miserably bad. The old Fort was occupied by the convicts whom he had sent there some time ago and were occupied in making a wall across the Island. They were locked up every night when they returned from their labour. About a week before we landed seven or eight of them took the long boat and made their escape to Hartland, and were never heard of afterwards.

"Wild fowl were exceedingly plentiful, and a vast number of rabbits. The Island was overgrown with ferns and heath, which made it impossible to go to the extreme of the Island. Had it not been for the supply of rabbits and young sea-gulls out table would have been but poorly furnished, rats being so plentiful that they destroyed every night what was left of our repast by day. Lobsters were tolerably plenty, and some other fish we caught. The deer and the goats were very wild, and difficult to get at. The path to the house was so narrow and steep that it was difficult for a horse to ascend it. The inhabitants, by assistance of a rope, climbed up a rock, in which steps were cut to place their feet, up to a cave or magazine where Benson lodged his goods.

"There happened to come into the roads one evening nearly twenty sail of vessels. The colours were hoisted on the fort, and they all as they passed Rat Island returned the compliment, except one vessel which provoked Mr. Benson to fire her with ball, though we used every

20

argument in our power to prevent him. He replied that the Island was his, and every vessel that passed it and did not pay him the same compliment that was paid to the King's forts, he would fire on her.

"He talked to us about his contract for exportation of convicts to Virginia and often said that the sending of convicts to Lundy was the same as sending them to America; they were transported from England, it matters not where it was so long as they were out of the country."

Benson had turned the desolate island into a source of profit. Taking the convicts some twenty miles to Lundy instead of across the Atlantic, for which the Government paid him, represented a considerable economy. At the same time he could use their labour to improve the island. He was busily engaged in draining the island and putting it under cultivation. The wall that the convicts were building was to separate the part not under cultivation from the remainder of the island with the purpose of confining the goats and deer to this part. He employed a small party permanently on the island including an Irishman, Jeremiah Magra, Andrews and an apprentice, Richard Ashton, who supervised the work of the convicts. Also on Lundy at this time was Captain Marshall of Barnstaple, a man very highly regarded in the district and who was master of Benson's vessel the *Catherine*. The Captain was there to carry out a special project that Benson had come over to discuss with him.

After a couple of days' stay on Lundy, Benson returned to the mainland with his guests, leaving his nephew Thomas Stafford in the charge of Captain Marshall.

Some three or four days after his guests returned to the mainland, the vessel, the brigantine *Nightingale*, which they had seen on their departure lying off Appledore Quay with convicts bound for Virginia, sailed, and Benson embarked on a plan that had steadily taken shape in his mind since the original idea came to him during the debate on the Insurance of French ships at one of his first attendances at the House of Commons.

Knapp House.

CHAPTER III

THE CREW OF THE *NIGHTINGALE*

The *Nightingale*, a brigantine of some 80 tons, was one of Benson's oldest vessels and soon would be unseaworthy. Benson resolved on a dangerous plan. He would load her with a cargo for the colonies, insure the vessel and cargo heavily, and then, taking off the cargo at Lundy, scuttle the old brigantine some way out in the Atlantic, claiming the insurance for both the cargo and the vessel.

He had planned the operation to the last detail, but to carry out his scheme successfully, without arousing any suspicion, it was essential that he should find a captain and crew whom he could trust implicitly.

The Captain was the man on whom most depended and Benson felt sure that in John Lancey he would have the right man. Lancey, who was twenty-seven at this time, was born in Bideford and "descended from a reputable family of that Neighbourhood." Well built, good looking and intelligent, he was of a somewhat quiet and serious disposition. His life had been spent at sea; a life he loved and for which he had been trained since boyhood. He shared the seaman's rough and ready pleasures, the robust fun of the waterside tavern and the enjoyment of a woman's company, and women found him equally attractive; but he found his greatest contentment on returning at the end of a voyage to his wife and two daughters at his home at Northam. Like most sailors he was fond of children and, only seeing his own occasionally, spoiled them utterly.

Lancey's wife was a relative of Benson, and Lancey himself had been in Benson's service as master of several ships for over ten years. The relation between the two men was much closer than usually exists between a merchant and the captain of one of his vessels. Lancey recognised Benson's ability and wide experience and frequently sought his advice and help in his personal affairs, and just now things were by no means rosy with him. Taken ill in the early part of the year, he had been out of employment for several months and his finances were running very low. He was, therefore, delighted when he received a message from Benson asking him to come along and discuss the fitting out of the *Nightingale* for a voyage which Benson was planning in a month or so.

The meeting of the two men was most cordial. At first the conversation touched on family and personal matters, but presently Benson brought up the question of fitting out the *Nightingale* for the proposed voyage. He remarked that the vessel had seen a good many years' service and needed a great deal done to her before she would be fit for sea. Lancey agreed.

Benson them remarked in a half humorous manner that the best thing for him would be to insure her heavily and then take her to sea and scuttle her. He paused at this and looked quizzically at Lancey; getting no response he said in a serious and thoughtful way that it was quite a sensible idea and asked if the thought had ever occurred to Lancey, who, startled by the suggestion, hotly replied, "Sir I flatter myself you have never known me guilty of a bad action since I have been in your service. Surely your mention of this matter to me now is only with a view to trying my integrity." At this Benson dropped the subject and returned to the matter of the repairs to the vessel. At Lancey's suggestion he agreed that the *Nightingale* should go to Instow quay where the work would be put in hand.

A week or so later Lancey received an invitation from Benson to join him and other guests for dinner at Knapp. The party included two Portuguese merchants with whom Benson had concluded a business transaction to the obvious satisfaction of both parties. Benson was in great form. The conversation ranged over a wide variety of subjects from the war with France and Spain and the hazards it brought to maritime trade, to the plague of rats on Lundy. Benson, always a witty and amusing conversationalist, entertained his guests with some libellous accounts of prominent members of Parliament. The wine flowed freely and the party ended in a merry mood.

As the other guests were leaving, Benson drew Lancey aside and asked him to stay. As soon as they were by themselves, Benson walked with Lancey to a pleasure-house in the garden. Here he returned to his idea of scuttling the *Nightingale*, outlined the plan he had in mind and urged Lancey to help him carry this through. Lancey told him plainly that if this was to be the condition of his continuing in Benson's service, he must seek employment elsewhere.

"They had drunk plentifully before, and Benson still plied him with more wine and more Arguments; upon which he touched upon a tender string; his Necessities, his Wife and two Children. 'Why will you', says

24

Benson, 'stand so much in your own light? Consider your circumstances, consider your Family; you may have an opportunity of making them and yourself happy.' His Argument unfortunately prevailed, and Lancey was undone. The Prospect of such large Advantages, found to Benson's strong and repeated assurance of Protector, gilded the Bait till Lancey swallowed it."

So, assured of the Captain he wanted, it only remained for Benson to find a crew. He signed on two young lads who lived very near him, Richard and John Sinnett. Richard was a sailor who had sailed in the *Nightingale* on her previous voyage, and his younger brother John, who had recently married and had never been to sea before, was taken on as ship's cook.

Benson entrusted the recruiting of the remainder of the crew to Thomas Powe, a rascally tailor who ran a shop in Appledore; a rough customer, Powe was a man of simple tastes – wine and women. He had often before made himself useful to Benson and had earned some easy money by carrying out shady jobs. One day in June, 1752, as Powe was drinking and joking with some women in an Appledore tavern, a young sailor, James Bather, came in. Seeing Powe there and owing him money, he decided to leave quietly, but Powe, who noticed him coming in, shouted across the bar and ordered him a drink. Bather immediately made excuses for not having paid his debt, blaming his lack of work that year. To his surprise Powe said that if he wanted a job he could find him one right away. "If you go in the *Nightingale* you shall make your Summer's work, your year's work double." Bather asked what he meant by that. Powe replied, "You shall go Boatswain of the *Nightingale* and have thirty shillings a month." The two men drank on this and Powe promised to arrange the matter that day.

Such sudden good fortune was unique for Bather, whose life had been hard and unhappy. He was born at Northam and when he was a very young child his father became involved in a brawl with another man. The Vicar of Northam attempted to make peace between them. Unfortunately for the Vicar, Bather was in such a fury that he not only beat up his opponent but seriously injured the Vicar. To avoid further trouble he fled the country leaving his wife to bring up the family as best she could. At the age of eleven, James Bather was sent to sea, and during the next few years he served in a number of vessels, including the *Benson Galley*, which fought the French as a privateer. At the age of twenty, in 1747,

James Bather married and again he was dogged by bad luck. His young wife died in childbirth leaving him an infant daughter to care for. Such was Bather's story. At twenty-five he was soured, suspicious and scheming.

The day after his chance meeting with Powe in the tavern, he went along to Powe's tailor shop where he was introduced to Captain Lancey, and was signed up as Bosun of the *Nightingale* for her voyage to Maryland.

One by one Powe found the rest of the crew. John Lloyd as mate and Anthony Metherall as second mate, Francis Shackestone as a sailor and two cabin boys, Thomas Sharpe and Thomas Husbands.

The *Nightingale* at this time lay at Instow Quay undergoing repairs by the shipwrights. James Bather, assisted by Richard Sinnett and a party of seamen rigged the vessel to the Boathide at Bideford to load cargo for the voyage. Here they took aboard some 350 bushels of salt and waited about three weeks for the remainder of the cargo. In the meantime they rigged a platform over the cargo space in readiness for some convicts expected from Exeter Gaol who were to be transported to Maryland.

When all was ready to load, Captain Marshall, master of Benson's vessel the *Catherine*, with three or four of his crew came aboard to assist. Benson himself was at the Boathide to supervise. Calling Richard Sinnett, the seaman, he pointed out, "a hogshead of dry goods," and told him to stow it away out of sight of the Excise Officers. After the officers had examined the cargo, loading began. On the top of the salt, already in the hold, they stowed bales of locally made woollen cloths, Irish linen, pewter and brass-ware and, finally, the "hogshead of dry goods" that Sinnett had hidden from the Officers.

Water and provisions sufficient for the voyage were taken board. In his account of the voyage, James Bather gives full details. There were 27 hogsheads of water besides an old iron bound hogshead with three heads to it, which had been used for smuggling by filling one part with water and the others with tea. The provisions included beef, pork, peas, a cask of oatmeal and a small cask of molasses and two thousand weight of bread; in addition they took aboard two barrels of strong beer and two hogsheads of cyder "for us to drink instead of small beer." Two hogshead of tobacco, each of seven hundredweight were stowed aboard and a further six hundredweight in the bread room.

Although the provisions were enough for the voyage to Maryland, Bather notes that the ship's stores were far from adequate. The *Nightingale* had only two anchors instead of the three she should carry; only one 6 inch hawser which was not big enough for her by two inches, and two worn out junks spliced together, which were fit only for mooring in a sheltered harbour. She carried no spare sail; the ones in use were so old as to be scarcely fit for coasting.

All the cargo and the stores for the voyage were now stowed. The Collector of Customs for Bideford with the Deputy Controller came aboard with the Bill of Lading and the "Master's Report Outwards" for Lancey's signature. (There was a staff of 25 Customs Officers at Bideford, which gives some indication of the ceaseless flow of shipping in and out of the port at this time.) Lancey received them in his cabin and read over and signed the Bill of Lading.

"Outwards Port of Bideford ... in the ship *Nightingale* of Northam, British built of particulars all British about 70 tons with ten men and none else besides Jno Lancey, a British man, master for this present voyage to Maryland in America.

Loose 365 bushels of Spanish salt ... on account of Alexander Ley.

T.B. 1 : 4 4 boxes cutlery ware
     1 : 2 2 casks haberdashery
     1 : 17 17 bales containing Broadcloath, Stockings,
                       Duffles, Kerseys, Serges
     1 : 5 5 casks nails ... one ton
     1 1 hogshead cordage
     1 1 box ... Lace and Silks
     1 : – 1 box ... Hatts
     1 : 7 7 bales ... Irish Linen
     1 : 6 6 hamper ... wrought Pewter
                            on account of Thomas Benson Esq."

Lancey then completed his Master's Report Outwards which was witnessed by the two officers.

"I do swear that the entry above written now and subscribed by me is a just report of the name of my ship built of (————), numbers and country of mariners, the present master, voyage and that it further contains a true account of my lading with further marks, numbers quantity and of particulars of all Goods and Merchandises in my ship to the best of my knowledge and that I am not to suffer to be unladed or unshipped in any part of Great Britain any certified goods which I have on board, nor take in any more goods for the present voyage without duly entering and adding the same to this report.

So help me God.

John Lancey.

Sworn before us the 27th day of July 1752.
Richard Parminter, Collector
P. Gregory, D. Comptroller."

Finally, the convicts brought from Exeter by Mr. Manley, Keeper of the Gaol, came aboard; twelve men and three women, ragged and hungry looking wretches; the men chained in pairs and the three women manacled together. They were herded below on the newly built platform, rigged over the cargo space and battened down (Lancey in his account states that there were fifteen convicts, Bather, however, claims that there were originally sixteen, but one of them, a skilled carpenter, was sent to Lundy to work on the Island.)

As soon as the Insurances were completed, Benson sent for Lancey and gave him his final orders. The *Nightingale* moved into the pool of the Port of Barnstaple where, to quote Lancey "every ship bound Foreign ride at anchor to wait for a fair wind." Here they were joined by Ann Stoar, a servant woman who was to be taken off at Lundy, "she being a very useful woman and that understands to make rabbit nets" and by John Sinnett, the cook, who brought with him a supply of fresh vegetables. (Bather maintains that Ann Stoar was a convict.) John Sinnett, simple, honest and plain spoken, is the most lovable character of the *Nightingale* crew; recently married he was leaving his wife and home to go to sea for the first time in his life.

CHAPTER IV

THE VOYAGE OF THE *NIGHTINGALE*

On Tuesday the 28th July 1752, the *Nightingale* sailed from the Pool of Barnstaple. Benson watched her departure from the grounds of Knapp House.

In the account of the voyage given by Captain Lancey, he states that he sailed "in order to pursue my intended voyage to Maryland, but the wind beginning to blow very hard from the westward on Thursday about noon, I anchored in the Road of Lundy, thinking it more advisable than to bear up for Kingroad or some port in the Bristol Channel, which I must have inevitably done."

Bather gives a very different version, stating that they crossed the Bar in company with a small sloop, but Lancey, not wishing to have the movements of the *Nightingale* known, drew apart as soon as possible and arrived under the lee of Lundy on the Tuesday afternoon. He records that colours were hoisted at the Fort on the Island, and they replied with a hoist in the *Nightingale*. The vessel came to anchor in the bay.

Powe and Captain Marshall of the *Catherine* had been sent ahead by Benson to await the arrival of the *Nightingale*. They had crossed to the Island with Captain Clibbet in a small brig, the *Vine*, owned by Benson. Captain Marshall's instructions were to go to Lundy where he would receive further orders. On the passage over, Powe put the suggestion to him that he should sail as passenger in the *Nightingale* to Maryland. Marshall replied that he would gladly go to Maryland if Benson would furnish a cargo for the *Catherine* but not as a passenger in the *Nightingale*. Powe put the proposition more plainly: "Supposing the *Nightingale* should miscarry and you have orders to draw bills on Mr. Benson, would not that do as well?" The Captain's reply was blunt. He would not go on any terms at all.

As soon as the *Nightingale* came to anchor, the two Island boatmen, Andrews and the Irishman, Magra, rowed out to the vessel bringing Captain Marshall who went below to Lancey's cabin. The two Captains drank a glass of wine together, and Lancey handed over a letter in Benson's handwriting addressed to "Peter Marshall." It was a very brief note ending cryptically – "Lancey will communicate some hints to you. T.B." Lancey then explained that he had received orders from Benson to land the cargo they had loaded at Bideford on the island. Marshall returned to Lundy taking with him the servant woman, Anne Stoar, to make her new home on Benson's island domain.

The boat returned next day, this time with Powe and Captain Marshall. Powe had been instructed by Benson to agree with the crew "in case the vessel should miscarry in her outward bound voyage to Maryland," how much money should be secured by each man by way of Insurance. Powe went to Lancey's cabin, where he and the Captain interviewed each man in turn. They were offered varying sums. Lloyd, the mate, accepted a note for £60, Shackestone one for £45, but when Bether's turn came and he was offered £40, he refused. He claims in his account that this proposition alarmed him at first, but "suspecting that they had villainous intentions, and considering that he would have no other security for his wages, his chest and his clothes decided to agree for fear of worse happening." He demanded a further five pounds and duly received a note for £45.

When agreement had been reached with all the crew, and Lancey had written out all the notes which Powe signed, Peter Marshall and Powe returned to the island. Well pleased with his day's work, Powe called for a bottle of wine to celebrate. He confided in Marshall that Benson had insured his (Marshall's) interest in the *Nightingale* for £60. The cautious Captain replied that he did not desire to have any interest in the *Nightingale* whatsoever, adding as he raised his glass of wine, that he wished it might be poison if ever he had any interest aboard.

Powe returned to Bideford with Captain Clibbet leaving the notes in the care of Captain Marshall who was to give them to the wives of the crew.

That night after dark the boat came out again to start taking off the cargo. Lancey gave orders to open up the hold and, so that the convicts should not witness what happened, he rigged a tarpaulin over the platform where they were accommodated. The boat returned to Lundy with as much of the cargo as it could safely carry.

The following night it made two more trips and took ashore all the cargo except the 350 bushels of salt. The next morning the *Nightingale* weighed anchor and sailed.

On the morning of Monday, August 3rd, the *Nightingale* was some fifty miles west of Lundy. It was misty and the sea calm. Through the haze Lancey sighted another vessel bearing towards them, the *Charming Nancy* from Philadelphia bound from Dublin. As they drew near her Captain hailed the *Nightingale*, and asked where they were from and how far Lundy bore from them. Lancey replied it was some fifteen leagues, and, as it looked dirty weather, advised the captain to keep to the westward of Lundy on the same course as they were steering. He had a fishing line thrown across to the *Charming Nancy*, and passed over a fresh cabbage and a bottle of wine as a present for her master, Captain Nicholson. Lancey, with all his crew on deck, waved to the *Charming Nancy* as she passed on her way.

As the *Charming Nancy* drew ahead, Lancey decided that conditions were ideal for putting Benson's plans into operation – a calm sea, bad visibility and very little wind, so the *Charming Nancy* would make slow progress and would be near at hand to rescue the crew. He gave orders to have the boat hoisted outboard ready for lowering. The boat was an extra large one that came from the *Catherine*, and the operation required all hands.

Lancey then ordered the sailors, Richard Sinnett and Shackestone, to go below and open up the hogshead that Benson had hidden from the Excise Officers. It was filled with small tar barrels and wads of oakum soaked in tar, which the two men spread over the sail in the hold.

Sinnett's next job was to cut a hole in the bulkhead separating the bread room from the hold. He swung his hatchet clumsily, cutting his leg and James Bather finished off the job. All was now ready to set the vessel on fire.

Lancey ordered Bather to bore a hole in the ship's bottom. The water gushed in with such speed that he plugged the hole with a marling spike while he went up on deck to see how far the *Charming Nancy* had drawn away. Going to Lancey's cabin he found the Captain with Lloyd, the mate, helping to dress Richard Sinnett's cut leg. Lancey started to sort out his personal effects and made the mate a present of one of his coats of blue broadcloth with brass buttons. Bather said he was very short of clothing and suggested that Lancey might give him something too, rather than leave his things behind to burn. he received a brown broadcloth coat and a green waistcoat both with brass buttons, and to go with these, a check shirt. Richard Sinnett was given a pair of black ribbed stockings.

All was set for the final act. Bather went down to the bread store and, putting a lighted candle through the hole he had made into the hold, set fire to the wads of tarred oakum. He then withdrew the marling spike which plugged the hole in the ship's bottom.

As the smoke began to pour out of the hold, Captain Lancey rushed up on deck and shouted down to the convicts in the hold, demanding to know what they had done and accused them of setting the ship on fire. The convicts protested their innocence, but Lancey roared back that they had ruined him and shouted out orders to lower the boat.

The bewildered convicts were put into the boat first, followed by the crew. Lancey still roared out accusations at the convicts as the flames leaped up from the hold. Bather made a show of attempting to control the fire. To the simple young John Sinnett, on his first sea voyage, it must have seemed an exciting adventure.

Captain Nicholson from the *Charming Nancy* saw the flames and smoke coming from the *Nightingale* and altering course, came back to give assistance. Coming upon the boat he took the convicts and crew aboard. Lancey immediately expressed his wish to make a further attempt to put out the fire, and the Captain ordered his helmsman to steer toward the burning ship. As they approached, Lancey felt that it was his duty to tell Captain Nicholson that the *Nightingale* had gunpowder aboard. The Captain replied, no doubt as Lancey had anticipated, that if she was carrying gunpowder, he would not bear down on her for five thousand pounds, and directed the *Charming Nancy* back to her original course.

After they had been aboard some three or four hours, the brigantine *Endeavour*, bound from Clovelly to Milford Haven, came up to them and seeing the flames in the distance hailed them to ask what ship was on fire. Nicholson replied, "The *Nightingale*, John Lancey, Master, from Bideford, bound for Maryland." Lancey, who knew the master of the *Endeavour*, Captain Cook, asked him if he could carry the convicts and his crew to Milford Haven. Captain Cook agreed.

There was little wind that night and the *Endeavour* made small progress. At two o'clock in the morning Lancey, who was still on deck, could see the flames on the *Nightingale* now burning right down to the water line.

The next morning the wind coming round to the North made the passage to Milford Haven slow and difficult. Lancey worried as to what he would do with the convicts on arrival at Milford Haven, pointed out their miserable plight to Captain Cook and persuaded him, as he had not enough water on board, to carry them to Clovelly where they arrived early on Wednesday morning. Here Lancey hired a boat, and crossing the bar in the afternoon, landed his party at the Boathide. After they had locked the convicts up securely in a barn at Knapp House, Lancey went to report to Benson. His account of this is interesting. "I thought it was my duty to deliver the convicts to my Merchant Esquire Benson, which I accordingly did; and also acquainted him of the unfortunate accident that had happened to his Ship, for which he expressed a very great concern."

Benson's Cave

CHAPTER V

BATHER TALKS TO BENSON'S RIVAL

The swift return of Lancey and his crew took Benson by surprise. Suspecting that his plans had miscarried he greeted Lancey coldly and was only slightly re-assured by the Captain's report. Tense and apprehensive, he questioned Lancey minutely on every detail. How much did the convicts see? What had Lancey told Captain Nicholson and Captain Cook about the cause of the fire? Did the Captain accept his story?

Only when he had probed every possibility was Benson satisfied that all was well. Pouring out two glasses of wine he congratulated Lancey on a job well done. Then he summed up the position and planned the next steps that Lancey must take. There was no evidence at all as to the cause of the fire and no proof that the *Nightingale* had been scuttled. Only the crew knew the truth of the affair and every man had a financial stake in its successful outcome. There was a possible risk that they might let out some of the story to their families, so as quickly as possible they must all swear an affidavit declaring that the *Nightingale* was lost by accident. This would have to be done in any case before they could claim the insurance, and no man would get a farthing from Benson till he had signed.

He then in great detail went over the story that Lancey must swear to as being the true reason for the loss of the *Nightingale*. Benson assured the Captain that he had nothing to fear and that his influence would protect him from any possible trouble.

On the following afternoon, Thursday, August 6th, Captain Lancey together with Lloyd, the mate, Anthony Metherall and James Bather, called at the office of Narcissus Hatherly, the Public Notary of Bideford. Lancey explained that they had come to swear to a true account of the loss of the *Nightingale*. The sailors looked constrained and ill at ease in the lawyer's small office, and puffed at their pipes while Narcissus Hatherly cleared a space on his table, cluttered with letters, deeds and documents, and laid out with great deliberation several sheets of paper, pens and ink. By a tedious process of question and answer, he translated the sailors' nautical language into legal phraseology and drafted out a precise and orderly account of the loss of the vessel. It was a task that occupied the whole of that summer afternoon. When at last it was completed, he read the text over to them.

"I Narcissus Hatherly, of Bideford, in the County of Devon, Public Notary, duly admitted and sworn; Do hereby certify all Persons whom it may concern, That on the sixth Day of August in the Year of our Lord One thousand Seven Hundred and Fifty-two; and in the twenty-sixth Year of the Reign of his Majesty King GEORGE the Second. Came and personally appeared before the said Notary, John Lancey, Master, John Lloyd, Mate, Anthony Metherell, second Mate, and James Bather, Boatswain of the Brigantine *Nightingale*, Burthen eighty Tons or thereabouts, belonging to Thomas Benson, Esq. of Northam, in the County of Devon, Merchant: who did freely and voluntarily on their respective corporal Oaths, taken upon the holy Evangelists; protest and declare before me the said Notary, that they sailed in the said Brigantine from the Port of Barnstaple, on the twenty-eighth day of July last; loaden with Bale Goods, besides fifteen Convicts sentenced for Transportation, viz, Twelve men and Three Women, Bound for Maryland; and the next Day the Wind began to blow very hard at West, so that they could not make any Way to the Westward.

On Thursday the 30th of last Month, they though it most advisable to come to an Anchor in Lundy Road (rather than bear up for Kingtown, or some other Harbour in the Bristol Channel) that they lay in Lundy Road till Saturday Morning the first Instant, when they weighted Anchor, and set sail in order to pursue their intended Voyage, having the Wind then at North North West.

That the next Morning (being Sunday) the Wind came about to the Westward, so that they could make but little Progress.

And on Monday last, being the third Instant, about One o'clock in the Afternoon, being then, according to their reckoning, about eighteen Leagues to the Westward of Lundy Isle; to the very great Surprise and Astonishment of all on board, it was observed by the Master that Smoke suddenly issued aft from the Hold, whereupon, the Master immediately ran forwards to the Place where the said Convicts were confined, imagining they might have contrived to have had some Fire to have been conveyed them; and upon lifting up the main Hatches, the Fire ascended with great Vehemence in the Master's Face; whereupon they used their utmost Endeavours to extinguish the Flames, but all proving vain and ineffectual, they then immediately got out their Boat, and every one on board betook themselves to it, or they must all have inevitably perished with the Ship.

That having been at Sea in the Boat about an Hour and a Half, they were providentially observed by a Brigantine, called the *Charming Nancy* George Nicholson, Master, of and from Philadelphia bound for Dublin; who seeing their Ship on Fire, and well knowing the extreme Danger and Distress they must be in, very compassionately came to their Assistance, and took them on board from their Boat wherein they then were; which must needs have sunk in a very small Time, being so very much overloaden by so great a Number as the whole Ship's Crew, and the said fifteen Convicts, in the whole twenty-four Persons: Or else if they could have had the good fortune to have kept their Boat any Time above Water, they must have perished for Want, having had no Time or Opportunity from the quick Progress the Fire made, to take out any Provisions, or save any Thing from their Ship, excepting a few Sea Cloathes (of little or no value) then on their Backs.

That about four Hours after they had been so taken on board by the said George Nicholson, there accidentally came up to them, the *Endeavour* Brigantine, from Clovelly, William Cook, Master, and took them all on board his said Vessel, who carried them into the Road of Clovelly; from whence they were by a Fishing Boat of that Place, brought in over the Bar at Barnstaple, and landed safe within that Port.

On Wednesday last, about Two o'clock in the Afternoon, of all which the said Master, Mates, and Boatswain, have made this their Protest; and they do hereby solemnly on Oath protest and declare, that the Ship *Nightingale's* so taking Fire, was purely accidental and casual, and proceeded entirely from some unforeseen Accident or Cause, which was not in their Power to hinder or prevent; and not from any Carelessness, wilful Neglect, or Mismanagement, to the best of their Knowledge or Belief. And that the Loss of their Ship and Cargo, and every Thing on board, was a total and unavoidable Loss by Accident of Fire.

In Testimony of the Truth whereof, the said Master, Mates, and Boatswain, did thereunto severally set their Hands, the Day and Year first above written."

The lawyer administered the oath to each man in turn and each signed the affidavit. Mr. Hatherly then informed them that it was too late for him to stamp the document that evening, but he would do this in the morning, and would then send it to Captain Lancey's house. He explained that it would be necessary for each of them to sign again over the stamp.

Duly, the following morning, the affidavit arrived at Lanceys house in Northam. John Lloyd and Anthony Metherall came as arranged and signed over the stamp. But James Bather did not turn up. The document awaited his signature.

Bather had gone that morning to Barnstaple. It was Friday, market day, and the town was busy with farmers and country folk crowding its narrow streets. Then, as to-day, the inns and ale-houses did a brisk trade, for here the farmers met their friends or settled a deal over a glass of ale. The news of the burning of the *Nightingale* had already spread through North Devon, and Bather found a ready audi nce in the taverns eager for a first-hand account and willing to buy him a drink in order to hear the fullest details of the story. No doubt too much drink made him incautious in his remarks, perhaps, too, there was already some suspicion and a great deal of local gossip as to the cause of the fire. At any rate the news of Bather's presence in Barnstaple was speedily conveyed to a certain Mr. Matthew Reeder, a leading Barnstaple merchant and a rival and bitter enemy of Benson. Sending for Bather to his office he took him to the "Swan Inn" (now no longer in existence) where, plying him freely with wine, he discovered the true facts of the loss of the *Nightingale*.

Considering that he had so much to lose it is strange that so crafty a person as Bather, even if drunk, should talk so freely. Not only was his share of the insurance money at stake, but having played an extremely active part in scuttling the vessel, he stood in grave danger of incriminating himself. Lancey in his account of the affair gives a possible explanation – "One of the chief motives that induced Bather to swear so contrary to his knowledge was, that a Law-Suit depending between him and Richard Passmore, a coachman to Esquire Benson, was not accommodated agreeable to his Inclination nor Expectations; and a certain Gentleman of Barnstaple, a Mr. Matthew Reeder, (a sworn enemy to Mr. Benson) who knew of Bather's being in Barnstaple, thought no time so convenient to put his evil Design in execution, sent for Bather, and what with his canting insinuations, persuasions, and the promise of a great reward such as I am sorry to say it, as would purchase many poor ignorant and distressed seamen, as was the case with this poor unhappy fellow Bather; who at that time could not be supposed to have a Shilling. After this Mr. Matthew Reeder thought he had wrought sufficiently on him, told him he must go to Exeter to complete what he had begun, and there to receive his Reward, but was first to call at Bideford on one Mr. W—— K—— who did his possible with him, and promised him preferment, and any station in a ship he was capable to undertake. By which means this poor unguarded Fellow, at the expenses of his poor soul, was brought over to execute so villainous a Design, which must have proved the entire destruction of many poor Families if he had succeeded."

Whatever the means he used to persuade Bather to talk, there is no doubt that Matthew Reeder seized at once his opportunity for scoring off against his rival, Benson. Returning to his office he wrote immediately to the Insurance office at Exeter giving a full account of all that Bather had disclosed.

The next morning Bather rounded up his two deck hands, Saxton and Richard Sinnett. They had worked under his orders as Bosun, and being older, more experienced and shrewd in many ways, Bather had acquired considerable influence over them. He persuaded them to accompany him to Benson's house to ask for an advance on the notes that Powe had given them and to see if Benson would increase the amounts they were due to receive. He said nothing to Sinnett and Saxton, however, of his meeting with Matthew Reeder the previous day.

They found Benson in a very good humour. He smiled a welcome to Richard Sinnett and said, "So, Dick, the work is done too quick; I have just made an end to my Insurance." He enquired what he could do for them. Bather, as spokesman of the party, asked first for an advance on the insurance money due to them. Benson replied that before he paid them any money they must first sign the affidavit, but Bather played his hand boldly and said they refused to sign unless they were promised a larger share of the profits. Benson was not a man to be crossed, he flew into a rage and, telling them to get to hell, declared that they stood to lose more than he did by a refusal to sign the affidavit; he, being a wealthy man, could better afford to lose the eight hundred pounds insurance on the ship than they could afford to lose their share.

Realising that nothing would be gained by further delay, Bather advised the others to sign the affidavit and set off to call on Lancey. He announced to the Captain that he had come to sign the affidavit over the stamp as Mr. Narcissus Hatherly had instructed them. He told Lancey that he had got a new job and would soon be at sea again in a vessel belonging to Messrs. Chappels, Barnstaple merchants and rivals of Benson.

In his own account of signing the affidavit, Bather claims that he met Captain Lancey with Lloyd and Metherall and "being much in liquor these men persuaded me to sign a false and villainous Protest," but the next day, realising what he had done, he wrote at once to a Mr. Turner, insurance agent at Bristol, and to a Mr. Tozer, agent of Exeter, to inform them of the truth of his action. (This is a most improbable story as Bather himself admits that neither of these letters were received.) However much the recollection of his signing the "Protest" troubled his conscience, it did not deter him from signing again over the stamp two days later nor from visiting Powe, the tailor, immediately afterwards and collecting five pounds and two shillings as part of the insurance due to him of his "Note of Hand."

A few days later, Bather received a letter from Matthew Reeder, the Barnstaple merchant, telling him not to leave the district as he might be needed. According to Bather he hired a horse the very next day after receiving this letter and set off for Exeter. Here he called on Mr. George Coad, an insurance assessor, and in the presence of a clerk, who took down his statement, he made a full confession of the scuttling and burning of the *Nightingale*. The following day he was examined before Alderman Heath. To his dismay and indignation, instead of receiving the reward he had looked to, he was committed to the Southgate Prison in Exeter.

Lancey, unaware of Bather's confession, believed that Benson's plan had succeeded completely. All the crew had signed the affidavit, there was nothing to arouse the suspicions of the insurance agents and no cause for him to suffer any further anxiety. So he settled down to claim his share of the insurance and on August 9th wrote to Mr. John Williams, Merchant of Exeter.

"To Mr. John Williams, Merchant, at Exon

Northam, Aug 9th, 1752

Mr. John Williams,

I Cannot give a more melancholy Account than what hath happened to me in the *Nightingale*.

On Monday last about 14 Leagues North North East from the Land's End, we perceived a Smoke in the Ship, to the great Surprise of all on board; and immediately went down to see whether we could see it amongst the Convicts; but before I could make any Examination, the Fire was so fierce, that Humanity obliged us to let them loose to save their Lives.

The Ship was immediately so full of Smoke and Fire, that we could not venture down, so we opened the Hatches, when the Blaze ascended in my Face; we used all Means possible to extinguish it, but all proved in vain; so we were obliged to get out our Boat, having that, and no other Chance for our Lives; and had not a Vessel from Philadelphia, Capt. George Nicholson, for Dublin, come to our assistance, we must have all perished in her, having not above six Inches free Board; nor had we any Time to take any Provisions with us to support us, had the Boat subsisted.

Sir, I am sorry my Wife should be so indiscreet as to send for the Policy; for my own part, I had much rather it had been continued with you; and upon receiving Advice from you how to proceed in this melancholy Affair, shall remit the Policy with the Inventory of my total Loss.

I am,
>Your most obedient Servant,
>>John Lancey."

"To Captain John Lancey.
>Exon the 13th, 8 month called August 1752

I Have received both thy Letters of the 9th Current, and am much surprised to hear of the Accident that happened to thy Vessel; but before I can properly apply to the Underwriter, I must have thy Protest made at thy first landing after the Loss, and the Proof of thy Interest.

As thy Letter giving me Direction to do the Insurance was dated the 17th of July, and I wrote thee the 18th, that the 130 1. was absolutely done here; So I cannot but admire how any Thing came to be done at London. Expecting thy Answer, I remain,

>Thy Friend,
>>John Williams."

"To Mr. John Williams, Merchant, at Exon

Northam, Aug 23, 1752

Sir,

I have sent you with this Post, the Policy, my Protest, and my Affidavit annexed to the Invoices of my Loss, besides Fifteen Guineas advanced to the Sailors; which I imagine I shall be able to come at, but rely on your superior Judgment to make Application for me, as I am so much a Sufferer; besides sundry other Items I have omitted in my Invoice, which really were on board at the Time when I sustained this Loss.

John Lancey."

* * * * * * * * * *

The days passed pleasantly for Lancey, lovely summer days spent in happy idleness with his family. He enjoyed leisure and freedom from financial worry such as he had seldom known before. Soon he would receive his insurance money, but in the meantime he could enjoy himself in planning what he would do with it, what he would buy for his wife and daughters, how he would make their lives happier.

His peace of mind was to be rudely shattered. On August 26th, a day of violent gale when many ships were lost in the Bristol Channel, Lloyd called on him and broke the news of Bather's visit to Exeter. He told Lancey that Bather had accused him of wilfully destroying the *Nightingale.* Lloyd suggested that it would be prudent if he left the neighbourhood as quickly as possible.

Lancey replied that he believed the story to be mere gossip, that he was sure Bather would not do such a thing and saw no reason "to secrete myself a minute on the occasion."

With Benson to protect him there seemed little cause to worry.

CHAPTER VI

THE ARREST OF CAPTAIN LANCEY

The following Saturday morning Lancey strolled to Appledore where he called at Powe's shop. He discussed with Powe Bather's visit to Exeter and the possible results of his disclosures. Powe expressed his feelings on Bather coarsely and bluntly and dismissed the probability of any serious trouble arising, since it was only Bather's word against the rest of them, and there was no evidence to prove that the loss of the *Nightingale* was not an accident.

As Lancey was returning home he met Mr. Thomas Nott, one of the Northam constables, who was accompanied by a stranger. At a sign from Nott, the stranger spoke to Lancey informing him that he was the sheriff of Exeter's bailiff. He asked him if he was John Lancey and had been Master of the *Nightingale* and Lancey replied that this was so. The Bailiff then said that his Bosun against Lancey for destroying the *Nightingale* with intent to defraud the insurers. He produced a warrant, which he said the constable must put into effect for the arrest of Captain Lancey and the ship's crew.

Lancey was detained at the Swan Alehouse in Northam. (The "Swan" had been left to Benson by his brother Peter.) The news of the arrest quickly became known in the district, and very soon several of the crew surrendered themselves to Mr. Knapper, the Bailiff. The Bailiff consulted with Mr. Thomas Lake, Town Clerk of Bideford, who had been commissioned to act for the Prosecutor, Mr. George Coad, an insurance underwriter of Exeter.

Mr. Lake, after studying the affidavit that the crew had signed, was of the opinion that, since Bather had signed it jointly with the others, it would be proper to discharge all the crew. However, after long discussion, the Bailiff and Mr. Lake decided to hold Lancey, Lloyd and young John Sinnett, the cook, and to discharge the rest of the crew. The Bailiff permitted the three of them to return to their home for the night on their undertaking to report to him at the "Swan" the following morning.

As John Sinnett played no part in the scuttling of the *Nightingale* there would have seemed to be little justification for his arrest. Subsequent events show that the prosecution, counting no doubt on his youth and inexperience, relied on him to corroborate Bather's evidence. There can be little doubt that Bather himself suggested this course.

The three men surrendered themselves to the Bailiff the following morning and set off with him, about mid-day, for Exeter. The Devonshire roads were in a shocking condition and the party were glad to break their journey at Wembworthy where thy spent the night at the "White Hart." The following day they arrived at Exeter, where they were placed under a strong guard at the "Seven Stars" Inn at St. Thomas. They remained here for two days until, on the evening of September 2nd, they were brought before a bench presided over by Mr. Justice Bevis and were examined in turn by the Prosecutor, Mr. Coad. Lancey records that the bench "seemed to be prejudiced in favour of the Prosecutor, by giving their opinions so partially, nay, even to condemn us before Judgement."

At the end of the examination, the bench ordered that the three men should be confined in the same room in the "Seven Stars" and every precaution taken to prevent their escape.

While they were in custody here they gleaned news of Bather. Bennett, one of the guards,. informed them that Bather "after he had sworn to the wilful destruction of the *Nightingale*, expressed a very great concern for what he had done, and desired the Prosecutor to be candid with him, in letting him know, whether the Captain by his swearing, would receive any hurt; for, says Bather, He's an honest man. I would sooner die myself than he should be hurt, and at the same time the Prosecutor assured him, the Captain should receive no damage. The Guard also told them that "when Bather found he was to be sent to Southgate, which is a gaol for the City of Exeter, he expressed a greater concern than before, and said, had he known he would have been sent to gaol he would not have sworn; for he imagined he was to swear to receive his reward and be secreted, as though he had given evidence against prohibited goods."

For nearly two weeks Lancey, Lloyd and John Sinnett were confined in the "Seven Stars," until they were examined a second time before the bench presided over by Mr. Justice Beavis. The bench committed them for trial and Lancey and Lloyd were taken to the county gaol. The keeper of the gaol, Mr. Manley, was an old acquaintance, who had often come aboard Lancey's vessels bringing convicts for transportation, and it was he who had brought the convicts aboard the *Nightingale*. He treated them well and allowed them every privilege.

Young John Sinnett was not so fortunate. He was conveyed to St. Thomas' Bridewell where he was kept in irons.

It was vital for the prosecution to obtain corroboration of Bather's statement. Above all they wanted evidence that would incriminate Benson. Separating Sinnett from Lancey and Lloyd, and keeping him in irons, was part of the plan to persuade him to provide the evidence they needed. He was visited several times, while he was confined in the Bridewell, by George Coad and others, who tried both threats and promises of reward if he would corroborate Bather's statement. But John Sinnett remained staunch and loyal to his captain. It is probable that he truly believed that the loss of the *Nightingale* was accidental, and certainly his letters from gaol tend to confirm this view.

In November, 1752, some five or six weeks after he had been sent to the Bridewell, an Habeas Corpus for John Sinnett arrived from London. He was taken by coach to London, and as undoubtedly part of Mr. Coad's plan to get him to talk, had James Bather as his travelling companion.

Sinnett describes the journey in a letter to John Lancey:

Wednesday Morning

Dear Captain

This comes with my Love and Service to you and Mr. Lloyd, and I hope you enjoy your Health, as the Lord makes me truly thankful, I am at this Time.

Captain, I am heartily glad you are come to Town, I would have sent you a Letter to Exon, but they told me you was to come away the Monday after; but I found it to the contrary, and am glad you are come at last.

It was about Four o'clock in the Morning when I left Exon, and when I came in the Coach to take in Bather, he asked me to drink a Glass of Wine, which I had as soon seen the Devil, as have seen him at that Time. But I told him I did not choose to drink so soon in the Morning, so were came away all that Day, but he seemed to be sorry to see my Irons, but I did not matter that, it was my Desire to wear them; But the next Day he would walk out of the Coach sometimes, but I could not walk for my Irons, and so he would walk several Times: But one Time he was going out again, and Bather seemed to be glad, for he wanted to make Water; but when some of them went out of the Coach, Mr. Glose put his Head and whistled to Bather out of the Coach Door, and Bather did not go out, but pist out of the Door: I could not think the Meaning of it, but I put my Hand to the Coach Door, and asked them what they meant by it, for I told them it was not proper: So when I came out, Bather came out too, and my Mind gave me that they wanted to bring me into a Snare; for, I believe it was a Contract between Glose and him, for he would have us lie together; but I would not, nor did not, and told them if I did lie with any one, it should be in the Chamber with Mr. Brown and his Man, which I did; and when I came to London, Glose would have Bather and I hand-bolted together. But I told them that they should Hand-cuff me, but not with Bather, nor I was not, but lied altogether in one Room.

They seemed to be afraid of Bather, and kept a Man two Nights in the same Chamber, but I was Hand-cuffed. Glose would have us quarrelled several Times, but I had nothing to say to him say what he would; he seems to be sorry for what he hath done, he should not have done it, if he had not been persuaded by Redor of Barnstaple, and some of Bideford, he hath brought a Coat, and Waistcoat, and shirt, and says you gave it to him for doing the Thing.

Bather brought a Letter with him from Mr. Coad, to take to one Mr. Brown, Sheriff of this Place; and I saw him take it to him, and opened the Letter, or else it was not sealed; but the Gentleman looked over it, and would have Bather look over something in it: So the Gentleman asked whether he knew what it was, and Bather told him he did: As far as I could learn there was something in the Letter that Bather was not willing should be known; for the Day before we came in, Bather swore that his Pocket was picked, and that Glose had take a Copy of the Letter, and swore he would burn the Letter, for it would hurt him, and would give Glose a Note for something, but what it was I could not tell; Insomuch that Glose told him, if he would swear that, he would swear any Thing.

And Bather two Days before we came in, they hand-cuffed him, for they thought he had a Mind to get off, for in the Evening he changed his Clothes before he went to Bed.

Two days after I got here, I was examined at the Judge of the Admiralty's Chamber by a thin Gentleman, who asked me, Whether I belonged to the *Nightingale*? I told him I did. And who shipped me? I told him the Captain. And what I had a Month? I told him eighteen shillings as a Cook: And where I went on board? I told him in the Pool, and went over the Bar the 28th of July. And what was the Reason we went to Lundy? I told him the Wind was against us, and I heard the People say, they would rather go there, than they would go for Kingroad, and tarried there two Days, and then went away again. He asked me whether we did not take in a Bullock there? I told him that there was about a Maund of Beef the Captain brought aboard with him: And how many Times the Captain was on Shore? I told him twice; and whether the Mate was on shore? I told him, No: And what was the Reason we left the Woman there? I told him she could make Nets, and Mr. Marshall had her on Shore: And what Powe did there? I told him for his Health or Pleasure, or what it was I could not tell. And whether I knew what Number was on the Goods? I could not tell: And what the People was called on the Island? I could not tell: And asked me about the Winds, but I told him I never was at Sea before, and I could not tell: And asked me how the Fire happened; I told him in the best Manner I could; And whether I saved any Thing; I told him a Shirt and a Pair of Stockings.

I told him all the Truth in the best Manner I could; he asked me if we saw Mr. Benson after we went over the Bar? And I told him we did not; And what I did after we went home again, whether I went to my trade? I told him, No, for I looked after the Transports some time after I went home, at so much a week till the Time I was taken up. I told him they did not take me up, for I went freely to them.

John Sinnett."

After his examination, John Sinnett was committed to Newgate Gaol, the foulest prison in London, notorious for its filth, disease and wretched conditions. However, he had no longer to put up with the company of James Bather whom he found so distasteful.

On Friday, 1st December,m 1752, Bather was examined before Sir Thomas Salisbury, Judge of the High Court of Admiralty, and, after he had made a full statement on the loss of the *Nightingale*, he was jailed in the Poultry Compter.

At the beginning of December, Mr. Manley, the keeper of Exeter Gaol, informed Lacey that he had received an order to take both him and Lloyd to London. On the morning of December 7th the party set forth. Lancey and Lloyd accompanied by Mr. Manley rode in a Post Chase with a guard of two mounted on "brave geldings." Oddly enough the guards were both one-armed men but were somewhat compensated for this by carrying a brace of pistols apiece. They travelled as far as Axminster where they paused for the night. Here they met Mr. Gloucester, the keeper of the Southgate Prison in Exeter, where Bather had been confined. (Mr. Gloucester is obviously the "Mr. Glose" referred to in John Sinnett's letter.) He was returning to Exeter after escorting Bather and Sinnett to London.

Mr. Gloucester gave them news of Bather and Sinnett and, according to Lancey, "told us that Bather several times on the Road had attempted his Escape; but by timely assistance of his Guard was detected and prevented; and to prevent any more Attempts of the kind, they put him in Irons, and in that manner brought him to London; but he (Gloucester) said that Sinnett behaved very decent and orderly during the Time they travelled together."

The rest of the journey passed without incident and on Sunday, 19th December, they arrived in London where they lodged at the Saracen's Head in Friday Street. Here they remained for about a week. Thanks to his old friendship with Mr. Manley, Lancey was permitted to take walks along the Mall. He visited the theatres at Covent Garden and Drury Lane (In the repertory of Drury Lane that week was a performance of "The Beggars Opera" by the Barnstaple poet, Gay. It is a pleasant speculation to think that Lancey may have seen this.)

After they had been in London a few days, Lancey and Lloyd were examined before Sir Thomas Salisbury, Judge of the Admiralty. Lancey gives an account of his Examination:

"Quest: By whom was I shipped, and when?
Ans: By Thomas Benson, Esq.: my Merchant, but cannot be positive to the Day.
Quest: What was your Cargo?
Ans: Bale Goods, ditto in Cask, and several Boxes of Cutlery Wares etc.
Quest: When did you sail, and how was the Wind?
Ans: On Tuesday the 28th of July last; Wind to the Westward.
Quest: When did you get to Lundy, and your Reason for going?
Ans: On the Thursday following about Noon; the Wind still to the Westward, and blew strong, prevented my getting there sooner; and thought it more advisable to go there than for Kingroad, or any other Place in the Channel.
Quest: What did you put Ann Stoar on the Island for, and by whose Order?
Ans: As she understood to make Rabbit Nets, and there being a great Plenty of Rabbits on the Island, my Merchant thought her a very useful Woman, and was ordered by him to put her on Shore.

Quest: When did you sail from Lundy, and what Time of the Day?

Ans: Saturday about Eight o'clock in the Morning. Wind at N.N.W. which was the first Time the Wind invited.

Quest: Did you land nothing at Lundy during your Stay there but the Woman?

Ans: Nothing at all.

Quest: When did your Ship take Fire, and how?

Ans: On Monday, the 3rd of August last, about one o'clock, as I was going down to take off that Day's Journal, I perceived a prodigious Smoke proceed from the Hold; I went immediately on Deck, and to the Place where the Convicts were confined; imagining they might have had some Fire conveyed them, but they declared they had none: I then raised the Tarpaulin, and the Flames ascended in my Face. We were then obliged to get out our Boat, or must have perished with the Ship, we did our endeavour to extinguish the Fire but to no Purpose.

Quest: What side was your Boat?

Ans: The Larboard Side.

Quest: I mean to Windward or Leeward?

Ans? To Windward.

Quest: Is it customary to get a Boat out to Windward?

Ans: No, but there was but little Wind, and the Ship was almost upright, and the Runners and Tackles that side, that we got her out with as much Ease as we could the other, nor should we have had Time to get her out to Leeward had we tried.

Quest: How long was you in your Boat before you got on board the Philadephia Ship?

Ans: About an Hour and a Half.

Quest: How long was you on board that Ship?

Ans: About two or three hours.

Quest: Where did you go then?

Ans: On board the *Endeavour* Brigantine, Capt. William Cook, who carried us into the Road of Clovelly.

Quest: What became of the Convicts?

Ans: I agreed with a Man to carry myself, Sailors and them into the Port of Barnstaple, where we came safe on Wednesday.

Quest: What became of the Convicts then?

Ans: I discharged my Duty by delivering them to my merchant."

In the course of the Examination it was plainly put to Lancey that if he would provide evidence against Benson he would be granted his liberty and no charges would be brought against him, and he was given time to think this over. It was a hard decision to make. Lancey knew that if he was brought to trial and found guilty the punishment would be death, or at the best transportation for life. To his credit he chose the harder way, he refused to betray his employer, to turn King's evidence and faced whatever trouble lay ahead. And so, on Monday, December 18th, Captain Lancey and Lloyd were committed to Marshalsea Prison to await their trial.

Two days later Thomas Powe was arrested at his shop by Mr. Thomas Stone, the Deputy Marshall. With a guard of three men they set off for Exeter where he was kept under a strong guard at the "White Horse" Inn. On Christmas Day, 1752, accompanied by Stone, he left Exeter for London. During the journey Stone persistently questioned him about the *Nightingale* affair, but Powe refused to be drawn. Stone advised him to trust himself to a Mr. Brown when he arrived in London. He described Mr. Brown as a gentleman from "whom he would meet a kind Reception, his Business soon despatched, and well paid for his Labour." Powe enquired who the hell this Mr. Brown was, and was informed that he was an agent for the Insurers. Powe replied in his usual coarse phrases, that he knew nothing of this Mr. Brown, and would not swear any statement for whatever bribe he might offer.

On the Thursday morning, the 28th December, Powe and Stone arrived at Stockbridge, and while they were having breakfast, an acquaintance of Stone's joined them and told Stone that he had just returned from the "Saracen's Head" in Friday Street, where he had been in the company of Lloyd, the mate of the *Nightingale*. He said that Lloyd had turned King's Evidence and that the Captain had been committed to Marshalsea Prison. Stone was delighted with this bit of news, and seized the opportunity to rub in to Powe that this was just what he had predicted would happen.

That afternoon they met by chance another traveller returning from London, who informed them that both Lancey and Lloyd had been committed to gaol. Powe was convinced that the first story was deliberately told to put him off his guard and cause him to turn evidence.

Powe and his escort arrived in London on January 1st, 1753. he was kept under guard at "St. Paul's Head," Carter Lane, and Stone gave the guard orders that he was to receive no letters that he (Stone) had not first examined.

Two or three days later Stone asked if he would have any objection to drinking a bottle of wine with some gentlemen who were interested in the *Nightingale's* policy, adding that the gentlemen would like to ask him a few questions concerning the *Nightingale*. Powe refused the invitation in characteristic manner and the meeting did not take place.

On Friday, 5th January, Powe was examined by the Register and Mr. Brown, the Insurers agent, before Robert Chapman, Judge of the High Court of Admiralty, at Doctor's Commons. Although no committal order was made he was taken to Marshalsea Gaol the following day. His commitment order, was made on March 3rd, nearly two months later.

"George, the Second, by the Grace of God, of Great Britain, France and Ireland, King, Defender of the Faith. To the Marshal of our Gaol of the Marshalsea, in our County of Surrey, greeting.

"We command you that by these Presents, you do receive into your Custody from the Marshall of our Admiralty of England, the Body of Thomas Powe, otherwise Poe; charged upon Oath, with counselling, aiding and abetting the wilful and felonious Destruction of the Ship *Nightingale* (whereof John Lancey was Master) upon the High Sea, and within the Jurisdiction of our Admiralty aforesaid: And him the said Thomas Powe, otherwise Poe, safely and securely keep in our said Gaol of the Marshalsea, until he shall by due Course of Law, and the Custom of our Realm, be discharged of the Offence by him committed, at the next Session of Oyer and Terminer, and Gaol Delivery of the Admiralty of England, to be held before our Justices assigned to deliver that Gaol of the Prisoners therein, being for Offences by them committed upon the High Sea, and within the Jurisdiction of our Admiralty aforesaid.

"Witness our Justice whose Names are hereunto subscribed this 3rd Day of March, in the Year of our Lord One Thousand Seven Hundred and Fifty-three; and of our Reign the Twenty-sixth.

Tho. Salisbury,
Geo. Paul,
Cha. Pinfold,
Rob. Chapman.

S. Hill, Register."

CHAPTER VII

IN GAOL

Despite the arrests of Captain Lancey, Lloyd, Powe and young John Sinnett, the prosecution had still failed to obtain the evidence they needed to support Bather's statement. Mr. George Coad and his colleagues, assisted, no doubt, by Mr. Matthew Reeder, the Barnstaple Merchant, were striving to procure by any means a further confession that would enable them to present their case. The prisoners were continuously subjected to every pressure and to promises of reward, but they maintained that the loss of the *Nightingale* was accidental, and utterly refused to give any information that would incriminate Benson.

Benson, shocked by Bather's confession, and by the arrests of Captain Lancey and the others, fully realised the danger in which he stood. It was vital that the prisoners should be released on bail so that he could then get them safely out of the country. He engaged counsel to make the application. In the meantime he visited their wives and families, giving them encouragement and financial assistance in their distress.

John Sinnett, imprisoned in Newgate Gaol, anxiously waited for hopeful news. Notoriously the worst prison in London, foul and stinking, Newgate was sordid to a degree impossible to imagine. Those awaiting trial and debtors were herded together with the vilest criminals. The newly admitted prisoners were received in a dark chamber known as the "Condemned Hold", where heavy manacles were clapped on both hands and feet of all comers until a financial bargain had been struck with the jailers. If the prisoner was penniless he was left manacled, and was only unchained at their whim. For centuries the position of head keeper had been recognised as a much coveted post of profit, and every form of extortion was practiced by the jailers and even by the prisoners themselves. They demanded "chummage" from all new arrivals, who were beaten or stripped if they did not pay up. The money they obtained was spent on drink in the dark and filthy drinking cellars below street level, which were an unfailing source of profit to the head keeper.

The wretched prisoners who could not afford to pay fees for better accommodation were kept in the foulest part of the gaol, known as the Stone Hold, an underground dungeon. According to a contemporary account "it was a terrible, stinking dark and dismal place situated underground, into which no daylight can come. It was paved with stone: the prisoners had no beds and lay on the pavement, whereby they endured great misery and hardship". Prisoners often went mad and many were mad when admitted, as the law of the day did not recognise such a thing as a criminal lunatic, and went raving around the wards. Prostitutes were admitted to such prisoners as could afford to bribe the jailers, and every sort of vice and debauchery was rife.

In these grim surroundings, some six or seven months after his arrest, John Sinnett received a letter from his wife telling him that Thomas Benson was arranging for Counsel to make an application for bail for the prisoners at the next Court. The letter brought hope at last into the dark stone dungeon of Newgate. Sinnett at once wrote to John Lloyd in Marshalsea Prison to pass on the good news.

"Newgate, Wednesday Five o'Clock.

Dear Friend,

I This moment received a Letter from my Wife, and she writes me Word that she saw Mr. Benson last Saturday, and he told her as sure as there is a God in Heaven, that the Gentlemen were all ready to appear as soon as he had an Answer from his Proctor, when there is a Court held, which he expected by the Sunday's Post, which I wish he did, by the Captain's Letter, and I hope by this Time they are on the Road, God send they may.

From your sincere,
and hearty Friend,
John Sinnett.

Give my Service to the Captain and Powe; I return him Thanks for his last Favour; all Friends are well at home.

Pray send an Answer to this."

Marshalsea, where Captain Lancey with Lloyd and Powe were confined, was a prison for pirates and debtors. Conditions here, though shocking by any modern standards, were far better than at Newgate. However, their relief on learning that Benson was applying for bail at the earliest opportunity was just as profound as John Sinnett's.

The application for bail was duly made. It was refused by the Judges and despair seized the hearts of the prisoners. Out of this despair, no doubt, prosecution hoped would come the confessions and the evidence against Benson which they wanted. The familiar tactics of threats alternating with promises of freedom were tried again.

Benson instructed Counsel to make a second application at the next session of the court, and again it was refused.

On July 3rd, 1753, some ten months after their arrest, Dr. Hay and Dr. Smallbrook made a third application for bail and presented a petition on behalf of the prisoners.

"To the Worshipful Sir Thomas Salisbury, Knt. and the other Judges of his Majesty's High Court of Admiralty.

The Petition of John Lancey, Master of the Ship, late the *Nightingale*; Thomas Powe, Merchant, in Appledore; John Lloyd, Mate of the said Ship; and John Sinnett Mariner, belonging to the same.

That your Petitioners have, upon the Oath of one Bather, who had owned himself perjured in the Case of the said Ship, suffered a long and severe Imprisonment, to the almost utter Ruin of themselves and their numerous families, who depend solely upon the Labour of your Petitioners for their daily Bread.

That your Petitioners have applied, but without Success, to this Court, in order to be bailed; and to the High Court of Admiralty in order to have a Day appointed for their Trial, but have not yet been able to succeed therein.

That your Petitioners have done all they can to remove every Impediment that can possibly lie in the Way of their Prosecutors, for their coming to a trial; but that the Design of their Prosecutors by their long and severe Imprisonment, is to endeavour to make them become Evidences against one another, which they cannot do without being guilty of the most atrocious Perjury.

May it therefore please your Worships, to extend the Justice and Compassion of this Court, to your Petitioners, and their suffering innocent Families, by admitting them to a speedy and fair Trial, by the Law of their Country; and thereby delivering them from an Imprisonment, which, in many Respects, is worse than Death itself."

This time the Court granted bail but in sums so vast that there seemed little hope for men of their limited means to raise such amounts. Lancey was admitted to bail in one thousand pounds and two sureties of five hundred pounds; John Lloyd in five hundred pounds and two sureties of two hundred and fifty pounds; and Thomas Powe in one hundred pounds and two sureties of two hundred and fifty pounds. They were granted seven days, until July 10th, to raise the bail.

John Sinnett was not granted bail. The prosecution tried new tactics to persuade him to talk. The Ordinary, or Chaplain, of Newgate, visited him and endeavoured to coax a confession from him. The Chaplains of Newgate were notorious for their devotion to the material things of the world and showed little interest in the spiritual welfare of their charges. The Ordinary hinted that it was hopeless to rely on Benson for help, that Benson was finished.

With only one day left to raise the amounts required, anxious, almost in despair, Sinnett wrote to Captain Lancey.

> "To Mr. John Lancey in the
> Marshalsea Prison
> July 9, 1753

Sir,

I Was this Day sent for in the Lodge by the Ordinary of Newgate, concerning our Affair, but I could give him no Satisfaction of Things I knew nothing of. He tells me it is over with Mr. Benson, so how it is I can't tell: He was desired by Brown, the Attorney, to come to him; but he was to blame he had not come himself, and then he might have given him his Answer. He asked me whether I was willing to be admitted to bail? I said I was; but he said, Suppose they require Bail we can't get? For Mr. Benson's Bail, he said, would not do. I thought the Ordinary of Newgate, had been a more honest Gentleman, than to concern himself in such an Affair; but I suppose they thought if I had known any Thing of it, that he was a Man to frighten me; but I thank God, him, not a greater Gentleman, I am not afraid of; for I will, and have spoken the Truth, and what would they have of me.

The Ordinary says, Where will I get Bail? I said to him, I believe to bail one would bail all; so I believe that I shall not be bailed: But I hope God will raise a Friend for me. I should be glad if you would write a Line or two when you receive this.

I sent Mr. Bellew a Letter three Days ago, but I have received no Answer: I should be glad when you see him, to tell him I want to speak with him; for I shall want Cash in a short Time; I have but One Shilling in the World, but I hope our Time is not long.

> I am,
> Your true Friend,
> John Sinnett.

Excuse Haste. The Lady's Name is Poll Cogdall."

(Poll Cogdall was a well known lady of the town in whom Lancey became interested.)

The following day the Ordinary again visited John Sinnett who still desperately hoped for news of the bail and for his release. The Ordinary said that the prosecution had now established the proof of their case. In a raid on Lundy, the cargo of the *Nightingale* had been found hidden on the Island. Benson was finished. The Ordinary suggested that Sinnet would be freed if he would tell all he knew.

That night, in the depths of despair, hoping for any word of comfort, Sinnett wrote once more to his Captain.

> "To Captain John Lancey in the
> Marshalsea Prison

Dear Captain

I Hope these Lines will find you well with your Friend, as I thank God I am at this Time; but under Trouble and Vexation, fearing we shan't get Bail to their liking.

I was sent for in the Lodge Yesterday by the Ordinary of Newgate again, he was desired by Brown to come, I can't think what they would have of me. I have declared what I knew of the Affair before I came to Newgate, and I can say no more if they kill me out of the Way. He saith that there were Goods found on Lundy; so there might for ought I know, but none I will swear that ever came out of the *Nightingale*. There might, for ought I know, be Goods found, what is that to me! If the Ordinary was to come again, he should come to me next Time. I suppose they want to put a Stop to the Bail, if they can, for I can't think the Reason they should be upon me so; I wonder they don't come to you as well as me.

Captain, I received yours with mine enclosed, you write me Word that our Friend is getting the Bail Bonds filled up by a Gentleman in the Country, I thought they should have been present, and I believe they must, or else we shan't be bailed.

Dear Captain, I must desire you or Mr. Powe, to send me a little Money, for mine is gone, and Darby Fair is next Tuesday, so that then there is always a Shilling a-piece spent; so I beg you will not fail.

Mr. Bellew gave me Directions to send to him, I have sent, but I believe the Letter never went: And if I should send a Messenger, I fear I should not find him at home.

I believe I have satisfied the Ordinary, so that he will trouble himself no more about the Affair, for, if he does, I can't resolve him; so that he may as well keep from me as to come. He tells me our Friend is not worth a Groat, but I wish I had all above.

Dear Sir, I must desire you not to fail sending by the Bearer, and write me Word what you think of our being bailed, and when it will be.

I am,

Your sincere Friend,

John Sinnett.

Newgate, Friday
Night Six o'Clock.

Please send what you can.

I have looked hard to Day for a Letter, but have none, I can't think the Reason; My Heart is ready to break to think we shall not be bailed; but I hope to God we shall; I hear that Dr. Paul spoke much for us in Court.

I beg you will write me Word what you hear from home and how it is. Remember me to Mr. Lloyd."

Despite all Benson's assurances and the frequent promises of protection, the money required for Bail was never raised. The prisoners remained in gaol awaiting their trial at the next Admiralty Sessions at the Old Bailey.

CHAPTER VIII

FLIGHT

For several years the Customs had been watching Benson's activities closely. In addition to the charge of smuggling tobacco in the *Grace* in 1749, still outstanding, there were now further charges of smuggling tobacco into the port of Barnstaple; in the *Nightingale* (Daniel Bird, master) on September 19th 1750 and in the *Britannia* (John Lancey, master) on the 16th November, 1750. Two writs of Scire Facias in the case of the *Nightingale* had been served on Benson and he had entered into bonds for duty and penalties, one for £1,153 on 25,000 pounds of tobacco and the other for £1,660 on 36,000 pounds of tobacco. A further six writs had been served on him in the case of the *Britannia* totalling £4,584 on some 99,000 pounds of tobacco. Altogether Benson stood in debt to the Crown for the sum of £8,229.

Writs of Scire Facias, now obsolete, issued by the Court of Exchequer, placed the onus upon the defendant to establish his innocence and show just cause to the Court why the penalties should not be levied. The defendant was not sued for a year and a day after the issue of the writ and then, unless they could produce a "just cause", judgment was given against him. Benson's lawyer appears to have employed every conceivable legal loophole to postpone the execution of the writs and it seems probable that Benson also used his influence with the Sheriff of Devon. The first hearing of the case of the *Grace* took place on October 23rd, 1751, when Benson pleaded that he had in fact paid the duty claimed by the Customs on July 11th, 1751. The Attorney General denied this and the Court commanded the Sheriff of Devon to serve a writ to "cause to come on the eighth day of the Hilary Term twelve good and lawful men of the body of the said county" to serve as jurors. The Sheriff did not serve a similar writ, nor did the jurors appear, so the Court issued a similar command to the Sheriff for the jurors to appear fifteen days after Easter. Again the jurors failed to appear and only after the Court had issued five further commands, was the case eventually heard. The cases of the *Nightingale* and the *Britannia* were similarly delayed.

It was hardly surprising, therefore, that the Commissioners of Customs should show considerable interest in the burning of the

Nightingale. On September 14th, 1752, some two weeks after the arrest of Captain Lancey, the secretary to the Commissioners wrote to Richard Parminter, Collector of Customs for the port of Bideford, instructing him to forward copies of the bill of lading and all entries in the port books relevant to the *Nightingale's* last voyage. Benson was probably unaware of these enquiries and in any case already had enough worries to occupy his mind. On November 25th he set out with his family for London, taking with him two servants, one of whom, John Underwood of Appledore, later gave evidence of Benson's stay in London. The journey took seven days, an uncomfortable affair in those days of abominable roads and danger from footpads. For a short while the family lodged in Duke Street, Westminster, until Benson made arrangements to rent a house in Parliament Street.

His stay in London was, no doubt, desirable on a number of grounds, the frequent attendances he was force to make at the Court of Exchequer, the escape it afforded from the scandal which the *Nightingale* affair had caused at home, and for the constant contact that was necessary with the lawyers who were endeavouring to arrange bail for the prisoners. It is doubtful if the importance of his parliamentary duties played much part in coming to the decision to make this move, though he may well have been powerfully influenced by the help which his friends in the Government could give him in his present difficulties.

The year ahead was to prove full of trial and anxiety. Already troubled by the way the *Nightingale* affair had miscarried he was uncomfortably aware that the prosecution on behalf of the insurers of the *Nightingale* were working ceaselessly to uncover any evidence that would incriminate him. On January 12th they met with some success. John Adams, a sailor, and William Trust, a shipwright of Bideford, laid information against a certain Alexander Ley, a merchant of Northam, and formerly a master in the service Benson, for wilfully destroying the vessel *Snow*, usually called the *Ropeyard*, off Newfoundland in May, 1751, with intent to defraud the insurers. (This was the same Captain Alexander Ley who had triumphantly brought the French Privateer *Pierre and Marie* into the port of Barnstaple during the war with France and Spain.)

William Trust gave evidence that "he saw a large quantity of Bay Salt loaden on board the said vessel as for exportation, and within a day or two afterwards, he observed the Salt had been very much diminished, and that this deponent believes that the greater part thereof had been relanded and carried on shore and says that he doth believe the said Salt was lodged in a warehouse or cellar belonging to the said Thomas Benson Esquire at Boathead."

The loss of the *Ropeyard* off Placentia had occasioned no suspicion at the time. The insurance monies had been paid up without question and it was most unfortunate for Benson that the matter should suddenly be brought up now. That the *Ropeyard* should have been lost, one year previously, in similar circumstances to the *Nightingale*, and that the owner, Alexander Ley, should once have been in Benson's employ, could well have been coincidental. It was an undeniable fact, however, and plainly declared on the time of loading signed by Captain Lancey, that the *Nightingale* was carrying 365 bushels of salt on the account of Alexander Ley. William Trust's information, that he believed the salt off-loaded from the *Ropeyard* had been taken to Benson's warehouse at Boathead, was distinctly awkward.

The Custom's, too, gave him further considerable cause for anxiety. They were watching Lundy Island and the movement of his vessels very closely, and gave Benson every reason to believe that they were planning to bring charges of smuggling against him.

Despite the strain of these very considerable worries, it was necessary that Benson should keep up a show of unconcern. It was vital to maintain the wives and families of Captain Lancey and the other prisoners in good heart, and he assured them that they would soon be released and the charges dropped. If any member of the crew should lose confidence in him and turn evidence, corroborating Bather's story Benson knew that he was lost.

On January 29th his wife died suddenly. Her death, hastened perhaps by the strain of the last few months, was a bitter blow for Benson, and cruelly timed, but there was little time for grief. on February 12th he appeared once again before the Court of Exchequer to answer the writs against him for the charges of smuggling in the *Grace*, the *Nightingale* and the *Britannia*. On the advice of his lawyer, who had exhausted the means of delaying the charges any longer, Benson withdrew his pleadings. Judgement for the £8,229 was given against him.

Faced with the problem of having to find bail for the prisoners, to pay for their legal expenses, and to subsidise their families, the judgement awarded against him was a shattering blow. In addition to this he was to suffer bitter humiliation, for once the judgement became known, his house in Parliament Street was besieged by creditors anxious for settlement of their accounts. His baker, butcher, chandler, and wine-merchant, waited daily on his doorstep and Benson was driven to instruct his man-servant, Underwood, "to acquaint such persons that he was not at home". For the rest of his stay in London, until he left in June that year, he hid himself in the house. Underwood gives a pitiful account of Benson at this time, saying that, when he was forced to go out to attend to his affairs, he left secretly by the back door in the early morning and did not return till late at night. He did not even inform his family where he was going, in case the pack of creditors that hounded him daily, should track him down.

From every point of view the future looked grim indeed, but Benson took vigorous steps to retrieve his precarious position. In addition to his efforts to have the prisoners released on bail, he addressed a memorial to the Lords Commissioners of the Treasury. He petitioned on behalf of himself, the inhabitants of Lundy, and the owners, Lord Cartaret and Lord Gower, that the Island should be established as a lawful place for shipping and the landing of goods, and for approval to be given for him to build a pier on the Island for the shelter of small vessels and to facilitate the landing of goods.

The purpose of this memorial was, no doubt, to forestall the intention of the Customs to prosecute him for smuggling. He counted on the influence of Lord Gower, then Lord Privy Seal, and Lord Cartaret to obtain the sanction of the Commissioners of the Treasury.

The Commissioners, however, approached Benson's petition with caution and sought the views of the Commissioners of Customs.

"To The Commissioners of Customs.

March 12th, 1753.

Gentlemen,

I am directed by the Lords Commissioners of His Majesty's Treasury to transmit to you the enclosed memorial of Thomas Benson, Esq., on behalf of himself and others concerned in the Island of Lundy, which their Lordships desire you will take into your consideration and Report to them the state of the case therein set forth with your opinion what is to be done therein; and also inform their Lordships what you apprehend are the particular reasons for the Memorialist making this application.

I am, etc.,

J. WEST."

The Commissioners of Customs stated their disapproval of Benson's application in no uncertain terms.

"To the Commissioners of His Majesty's Treasury.

March 27th, 1753.

May it please your Lordships,

In obedience to your commands signified by Mr. West on the memorial of Thomas Benson on behalf of himself and the other Proprietors of the Island of Lundy, and likewise on behalf of all the said inhabitants of the said Island praying for the reasons therein contained that it may be put under some Regulation in respect to Trade, your Lordships directing us to take the same into considerations and report a State of the Case therein set forth, without opinion what is fit to be done therein and also to inform your Lordships what we apprehend are the particular Reasons for the Memorialist making this application.

We humbly report, that, since the receipt of Your Lordships' Commands, we have endeavoured to procure the best information we could on the several matters contained in the said memorial, so far as related to the Revenue, and having had recourse to the books and papers in our Secretary's Office, we find that in the year 1721, and for some succeeding years, when the Island of Lundy was in the hands of Mr. Richard Scores, who rented it from the Proprietors, several illegal practises were carried on there and considerable quantities of goods were seized by the Officers of the Customs, till a stop was put thereto by the said Scores leaving the Island; since which, we are informed the said island remained uninhabited and entirely neglected by the Proprietors. But we beg leave to inform Your Lordships that within three years last past, we have received from time to time, information that the smuggling trade has been revived there and that goods have been frequently landed on the Island, and Orders have been given to the Customs at the Ports of Bideford and Barnstaple to be very careful in endeavouring to direct and prevent the same, and in November, 1751, we received information that a cargo of tobacco had been entered at the port of Barnstaple for Morlaix in France, relanded in Lundy and afterwards brought back and thereby the Crown defrauded of the Duties, which being a matter of great importance we beg leave to lay the case before Your Lordships. On the 11th October, 1751, the ship *Vine*, John Clibbitt, Master, sailed from the port of Barnstaple, with sixty hogsheads of tobacco on board. The next day or the day after, she arrived Milford where she stayed till the 3rd November following, waiting as the Master pretended for orders, but being then told by the Officer of Customs that if he did not proceed on his voyage he would seize the vessel and cargo he thought it proper to sail from thence, and on the 7th day of the said month arrived at Barry in Wales to load coals. As it was almost incredible that a vessel should be able to perform a voyage from Milford to Morlaix, there discharge a cargo of sixty hogsheads of tobacco and come back to Barry in Wales, all this in the space of five days, it was suspected the Master of the vessel had landed the cargo at Lundy and therefore we thought it proper to send an Officer thither with orders to seize all tobacco he should find and although the said Officer was too late to seize the tobacco he was well convinced that a considerable quantity had been landed there a short time before his arrival, by the number of hogshead staves then remaining, the marks of which had been cut out except for one, on which was TB No. 12, and also by the quantity of waste Tobacco which lay scattered about. And the suspicions that the said Cargo of Tobacco shipt and entered out for Morlaix, and after being landed was brought back from thence is strengthened by the account we received afterwards that on the 13th November, 1751, 1,127 pounds of tobacco were seized at Appledore in the ship *Dolphin* belonging to the memorialist, and much about the same time, a seizure was made at Ilfracombe of a large Fishing Boat laden with cake tobacco, which, by the damaged part cut off, appeared to have passed through the hands of the Customs. And about the same time large quantities of Tobacco were found in Houses, Barns, Bushes and Hedges all of which were suspected to have belonged to Clibbit's Cargo before-mentioned, and to have been brought from Lundy, and we beg leave to observe to your Lordships as a corroborating circumstance of this Fraud. We are informed that no Tobacco is sent to France from this Kingdom, but what is brought by the company's agents, and this cargo pretended to be sent by the ship *Vine* was not brought so. But from further information just now received, we have reason to think the whole scheme of this Fraud will be fully detected, and that we shall be enabled effectually to prosecute the Persons concerned therein.

We further report, the Isle of Lundy, by its situation is very convenient for Smuggling, as it lies near in the midway between England and Wales, so that from thence goods may be run to either side of the channel with all the ease imaginable and especially if a pier was to be built as proposed by the Memorialist for the shelter of small vessels which are usually employed on such occasions and, therefore if this Island was to be established a Place for the ordinary Shipping and landing of goods, we apprehend that it would soon become like the Isle of Man, a magazine of Goods for illicit Trade; not is this our opinion only, but, as far as we can learn, it is the general sense of the Merchants residing thereabouts; and even considering the present situation of the Revenue with regard to the said Island, in order to suppress and put a stop to smuggling there, we think it might be proper for the present to appoint a Sloop or Cutter of about Forty Tons to be commanded by an Officer on whose resolution, Zeal and Fidelity, we could rely, from Experience already had, and who is well acquainted with the Coast and Trade carried on in these parts, to be properly stationed and occasionally as Wind and Weather will permit, to visit the Island of Lundy, to rummage for, and seize all prohibited and also customable Goods for which the Duties did not appear to have been paid.

Upon the whole, although we are not able to inform Your Lordships what may be the true motives of the Memorialist making this Application, we are of Opinion, as we have before observed, the Revenue will be exposed to great Frauds should the Island of Lundy be established a lawful place for Ordinary Shipping and Landing of Goods.

Which is humbly submitted.

etc.

Customs House,
London."

Certain phrases used in this report, "from further information just now received" and "as far as we can learn, it is the general sense of the Merchants residing thereabouts", are highly significant and indicate that Mr. Matthew Reeder, the Barnstaple Merchant, and other rivals of Benson were doing their utmost to bring about his downfall.

The Commissioners of the Treasury expressed their concurrence with the opinions expressed in the report, and also with the plan for stationing a sloop or cutter to keep watch on Lundy.

"To the Commissioners of Customs

10th May, 1753

Gentlemen,

Having laid before the Lords Commissioners of His Majesty's Treasury your report upon the petition of Thomas Benson Esquire in relation to the Island of Lundy; their Lordships have directed me to acquaint your that they approve thereof and desire you to present to them a proper person to command the sloop or cutter you propose to station on that Island.

I am, etc.

J. WEST."

Benson's plan for forestalling the Custom's prosecution for smuggling was frustrated. The consequences of his failure proved grave indeed. On June 27th he appeared again before the Court of Exchequer on nine writs of Scrire Facias. His lawyer offered no defence and judgement was given against him for £6,187. The previous fines against him had not yet been paid so the Court issued an estreat under which the Sheriff seized his estate at Knapp and other properties, as security for the debts to the Crown.

At the end of June he returned to Knapp. The days that followed were busy and anxious ones. He had daily discussions with his lawyer, Narcissus Hatherly, planning to save his estates from bankruptcy. In the hope of preserving some of his assets he appointed two relatives, William and Thomas Melhuish, as trustees. He made over to them his trading vessels and cargoes, and on August 11th wrote to Captain Hogg, master of the *Peter*, and Captain Salmon, master of the *Placentia*, both of whom were fishing off Newfoundland, informing them that in future they would receive their orders from the Melhuishes. As things were to turn out, this move of Benson's was to prove remarkably farsighted. perhaps, even in those dark days, he had a carefully worked-out plan for the future.

The seizure of his estates by the Sheriff made it impossible to raise the enormous sums necessary to bail Lancey and the other prisoners. The authorities were, no doubt, aware of this when they granted bail, for the Chaplain of Newgate had hinted as much to young Sinnett. Benson realised the acutely dangerous situation that his failure to raise the bail would create. Although the prisoners had remained loyal to him despite every temptation, trusting him implicitly for help and protection, once they realised that all his promises were worthless, they might well try to buy their freedom by turning King's evidence.

He made one last desperate effort to save the day. Relying on his influential friends in the Government, he threw himself on their mercy and once more petitioned the Commissioners of the Treasury in a memorial.

"To the Right Honourable Lords Commissioners
of his Majesty"s Treasury.

17th October, 1753.

The Memorial of Thomas Benson of Northam in the County of Devon
Esquire.

Humbly sheweth that whereas he standeth indebted to his nation in
several sums of money due on sundry Tobacco bonds now in the hands of
the solicitor of customs which have been put in execution and for which
the estates of Thomas Benson are now in possession of the Crown by an
Estreat, and the said Thomas Benson being desirous of paying and
securing the same humbly presents to your Lordships the following
proposals. (Viz.)

That the whole Estate contained in the Schedule herein annexed be
conveyed in Trust to two Gentlemen of indisputable good character for
raising the sum of £2,000 and to pay the same into the hands of the
Officers of the Crown on or before the 25th day of March next, and that
the said Trustees do also pay on or before March 25th then next
following, the further sum of £1,000, and then to continue every 25th day
of March following the payment of £1,000 until the whole debt from the
said Thomas Benson to the crown be paid off and discharged.

That the trustees to be named may be those that can repose due trust
and confidence for the just performance of their Trust, and as such the
said Thomas Benson names William Barbor of Lary in the County of
Devon aforesaid Dr. of physick and William Melhuish of Satterley in the
said county Barrister at Law and the Rev. Thomas Melhuish of
Witheridge in the county aforesaid Clarke, or any two of them as your
Honours shall seem meet.

That the said Thomas Benson will oblige himself by such deed of
Trust to execute everything in his power to enable the trustees to raise
money by mortgage, sale or otherwise of the said estate and that the
money arising thereby shall go to and be applied for and towards the
payment of the said debt due to the Crown as aforesaid and to no other
use, intent or purpose whatsoever to which the said Trustees will oblige
themselves in like manner.

That the Officers of the Crown do remain in full possession of the said
Estates, by virtue of the extent only to join with the Trustees in what is
necessary for raising of any part thereof by mortgage, sale or otherwise
as approved, and in case those several sums are not paid on or before the

respective times mentioned, then the office of the Crown to sell the estates or any part thereof and pay or apply the money arising thereby in discharge of the said Debt.

That the said Thomas Benson having an honest desire of paying his just due to the Crown on the several tobacco bonds and humbly and heartily makes these his proposals to your Lordships wise consideration and with great condescensions submits himself to your Lordships will and pleasure, thereby hoping to find such relief from your Lordships usual sanity and goodness towards himself and family (who must otherwise be totally ruined and undone unless timely aided and assisted therein) as to your Lordships shall seem meet, and your petitioner as in duty bound shall ever pray and

who am,

Your Lordships most humble and most obedient servant,

THOMAS BENSON."

Attached to this memorial was a four page schedule listing all Benson's properties which were estimated to realise £10,877 2s 4d.

Their Lordships of the Treasury, as before, sent his memorial to the Commissioners of Customs for their report. Unfortunately no record of their reply exists. There can be little doubt, however, that it was unfavourable to Benson, who realised that his last hope had failed, that he might soon have to answer for his part in the *Nightingale* fraud, and that this might well cost him his life.

One day, early in December, leaving Lancey and the other prisoners to their fate, he fled to Portugal.

CHAPTER IX

THE TRIAL AT THE OLD BAILEY

On February 25th, 1754, some eighteen months after his arrest, Captain Lancey with John Lloyd and Powe were brought to trial at a Court of Admiralty in the Old Bailey. Although still detained in Newgate, no charges were preferred against John Sinnett.

Lancey and Lloyd were indicted for "unlawfully burning and destroying the ship *Nightingale*, Thomas Benson, Esq., Owner on the High Seas, within the jurisdiction of the Admiralty of England with intention to defraud Robert Liddel, Samuel Toucher, George Rooke and Vincent Biscoe; and Thomas Powe as an Accessory before the Fact for counselling and advising to commit the same on August 4th, 1752.

Captain Peter Marshall from Barnstaple and most of the crew of the *Nightingale* gave evidence against their Captain, persuaded, no doubt, by Mr. Coad, that they would save their own skins by doing so.

The first witness to be called was Captain Marshall, according to a contemporary account of the trial.

Peter Marshall. I have been seven Years employed in the Service of Mr. Benson, who was Owner of the Ship *Nightingale*, and another called the *Catherine*, and have been employed as Master two Voyages in these Vessels, once in each. In the Year 1752, I was not Master in either of them, but was employed in fitting out the *Catherine* in the Spring of that Year. I had been sick, and Mr. Benson came to me and desired me to go as Master of the *Catherine*, and told me she was not to perform her Voyage. Some Time after that, he desired me to pack up a small Quantity of Goods for him, consisting of 90 Pieces of Irish Linen, some Hardware, Brass, and Pewter, which were shewed to the Custom-house Officers, and were entered at the Custom-house. After they were packed up and viewed by the King's Officers, they were taken out by Mr. Benson's Order, he himself being present, and Brickbats and Hay put in their Place. Some were put on board the *Catherine*, but put on Shore again afterwards and the Brickbats and Hay sent in their Stead. After she sailed, these Goods were packed up, in order to be shipped on board the *Nightingale*, but I was not there then, but Mr. Benson told me so.

Council for the Prisoner. This is giving an Account of a Conference between the Evidence and Benson. I don't perceive this was with the Privacy of any of the Prisoners.

Council for the Crown. We are going to shew the Goods were packed up to be sent on board the *Nightingale*, and after that were re-landed.

Marshall continues. Benson asked Lancey to be in the Room when these Goods that had been entered at the Custom-house, in order to be sent on board the *Catherine*, were unpacked and Brickbats put in, in order to be put on board the *Nightingale*. This was in Mr. Bensons long Room, about two Miles from Bideford. They were packed up in small Bales, twelve or sixteen Pieces of Irish Linen, and some Woollen. I remember nothing of Hardware or Pewter. This I saw, but did not see them put on Board. Mr. Benson sent me to the Island of Lundy, and gave me Orders to stay there five or six weeks, to look after the Affair, till I heard further from him, and to take Care to send his Nephews Home. Whilst I was there the Ship *Nightingale* came, which was the latter End of July; Lancey was Master of her, and Lloyd was Mate, I and three or four Men went on board her. We came there one or two Days before she arrived. After this, Powe told me he was sent by Mr. Benson, to agree with the Ship's Company, that in case the Ship miscarried in her outward-bound Passage to Maryland, he was to secure so much Money for them; but I did not hear the Agreement made. There was a small Bundle of Papers left with me, but I do not know the Contents. The Ship was then lying in Lundy Road. Capt. Lancey brought me a Letter from Mr. Benson, (he is shewn one) this is it; it is his own Handwriting; at the Conclusion he says, 'Lancey will communicate some Hints to you.' Directed to Peter Marshall, and signed T.B. Lancey accordingly told me, he had Orders from Benson to re-land the Goods that were shipped on board the *Nightingale*, on the Isle of Lundy. These were accordingly landed, and all buried under Ground. There were 15 or 16 Bales of Goods, and five or six Maunds or Parcels of Pewter.

Q. Who does this Island belong to?

Marshall. I don't know; but Benson rents it; it is near three Miles long.

Q. By whose Orders were they buried?

Marshall. By Mr. Benson's Orders, who sent a Man over with Hogsheads to put the Goods into when we buried them; as the Man that brought them told me. Lancey and Lloyd were not privy to the Burying the Goods; neither was Powe there, but was at their Landing them on the Island. Most of the Goods were on Shore before I came on board the second Time: I had been on board before.

Q. Who gave you the Bundle of Papers?

Marshall. Powe left them in the Window, he did not deliver them to me; and Thomas Salmon said he had an Order to have them from me, and I delivered them, and when Mr. Benson came on the Island, they were burnt immediately by him and Salmon in my Presence. This was after the Information was made.

Q. Were all the Goods buried that were on board the Ship?

Marshall. No, there came a Man of War along Side of her, and some of the Goods were hove over-board.

Q. What was the Conversation with Powe before you came to the Isle of Lundy?

Marshall. Powe asked me to go as a Passenger in the *Nightingale* to Maryland. I said, if I had a Cargo sufficient to furnish a new Vessel, I should be glad of the Offer. He said supposing the vessel should miscarry, and you should have Orders to draw Bills on Mr. Benson, would not that do as well? I told him I would not go on any Terms whatever.

Q. Did he say the Vessel should be lost?

Marshall. Not plainly; but I understood by him it was to be so. After the Goods were re-landed in the Lundy Road, we were drinking a Bottle of Wine together; he told me, Mr. Benson had insured for me 50 or 60 1. on board the *Nightingale*. I told him I had no interest on board her; and as I was going to drink a Glass of Wine, I said, I wished it might be Poison if ever I asked to have any Interest on Board. After this I went Home to Mr. Benson; he told me he had wrote to the Officer, to contradict that of my having any interest on board her.

Cross-examination.

Q. Was Lancey privy to the Hiding the Goods?

Marshall. I do not know that he was; that was done after the Vessel sailed. When Mr. Benson came on the Island, we had some Suspicion that the King's Officers were coming to search the Island; upon which they were buried; I was present at the Time.

Q. Did you see Lloyd when the Goods were packed up at Benson's House?

Marshall. I do not remember I did; I do not know he was acquainted with any of these Things I have been speaking of.

Richard Ashton of Lundy was the next witness.

Richard Ashton. I was Apprentice to Mr. Benson, and have been with his three Years; I was on the Isle of Lundy, and remember the Ship *Nightingale* coming into the Road there; she stayed about three or four Days; I went on board her, where were Marshall, Jeremiah Magra, and another Person, now on the Island, and John Sinnett; I was in the Boat, and they in the Ship; there were Bales of Cloth put out of the Ship into the Boat, and carried on Shore in the Island the first time; the second time we carried several Maunds of Goods; when we had them on shore we opened the Bales. This Coat, Waistcoat and Breeches, I now have on, were made of some of the Cloth we brought from on board the *Nightingale*; we put them into Casks, and hid them under-ground in the Island; Andrews and Magra buried the Pewter in the Rocks.

The next witness was Richard Sinnett.

Richard Sinnett. I was a Sailor on board the *Nightingale*, 'Squire Benson invited me to enter myself a Seaman on board her, which I did about 19 or 20 Months since; He told me to carry but very few clothes with me, for it would not be above three Weeks or a Month's Voyage; and that I should know my Business farther when I came to the Island; I assisted in loading the Vessel; that there were 17 or 18 Bales of Goods; there were some Bales on board on the Account of Captain Ley.

Q. What Conversation had you with Benson on this Account?

Sinnett. Before the Ship sailed, I was with him at a Place called Boathead; he told me there was a Hogshead of dry Goods, which were to be put out of the way of the Officers, who were to come there, which we put in the Rope-walk till after the Officers had been there; then it was put on board the *Nightingale*, and laid on some Salt, where also lay some Bale-goods; we had 15 Convicts on board. About the later End of July we arrived at the Island of Lundy, on a Thursday; the Wind was at the Westward, and we were two Days turning to it; we stayed there till the Sunday Morning; during our Stay there, there came a Boat on board from Lundy, with Marshall, Magra, and several People belonging to the Island. Powe and Lancey were in the Cabin, and called me to them; Bather was coming out when I came in; Powe gave me a Note, Shackstone was there also; I believe Lancey was gone out when Powe gave me the Note, and said, Here is a Bill for you, if the Ship should be lost in her Passage outward-bound to Maryland. The Note ran thus:

'I promise to pay to Richard Sinnett the Sum of 45 1. in case the Vessel is lost in her Passage to Maryland.'

He said, you never saw so much Money before, and the Voyage would not be long. He said, he'd deliver the Notes to Capt. Marshall, that he might deliver them to our Wives, in case we should come to any danger. He did not say when these Notes became payable, nor was any thing said about Insurance Money; the Notes were given after the Goods were landed; the Boat went with them two or three Times with 17 or 18 Bales of Goods, and five or six Maundes of Pewter and Brass; there were a great many Casks in the Hold, but what were in them I know not; there were Tarpaulins hung up before the Convicts on the Hatchway, that they should not see the Goods taken out of the Vessel. On the Sunday Morning we sailed from Lundy; the next Day, about 18 Leagues from Shore, we met a Brig from Philadelphia; our Captain hailed him, asked where she came from, and sent two Bottles of Wine and a Cabbage on board her. She steered with us; but was about a League-a-head of us, when Orders were given to destroy the Vessel.

Q. Who gave these Orders?

Sinnett. I do not know. When the Hole was boring in the side of the Vessel, Capt. Lancey ordered me to go to a Cask where was some Combustibles, and cut it up, and take out what was to burn the Ship; somebody had bored a Hole in the Side, for there was Water coming in when I went down, to do as ordered. I went and cut the Hogshead, and Shackstone and I cut it open; this was the same Hogshead that 'Squire Benson ordered me to put out of the Way of the Officers; there were in it, Tar-barrels, Staves, and Wads of Oakum dipped in Tar. Shackstone and I laid them abroad on the Salt. Capt. Lancey had said, when he gave me Orders to take them out of the Cask, that she would sooner be destroyed by Fire than any other way, and that now was as good a Time to destroy her as any; then he ordered some of the People to cut a Hole in the Bulk-head near the Bread Room; I went to cut a hole, and cut my Leg with the Hatchet; I came up and told the Captain my Misfortune, and could not do it. About half an Hour after this, the Ship was set on fire; then the Captain went fore and aft the Deck, and asked the Transports if they had set fire to the Ship? They said they had not. Then he ordered to have them

71

cleared directly, and the Mate was very industrious on clearing them; then we went all Hands into the Boat.

Q. Did you see Lloyd employed in any thing about destroying the Ship?

Sinnett. I did not. The Boat we got into was one Mr. Benson ordered for the Ship; tho' it was full large for that Ship. The Philadelphia-man saw our Boat coming towards him, and the Smoke arising, and we had fired a Gun by the Captain's Order. The Vessel came towards us. When the Combustibles were lighted, we all said it was the best Way to fire a Gun; and it was loaded about two Hours before by the Captain's Order. He said it was for the Ship that was ahead to hear us. We were taken on board the Philadelphia Ship, except some who tarried in the Boat along-side her two or three Days; after which we were landed by the Assistance of a Fishing-boat.

Q. When did you see Benson after this?

Sinnett. Two Days after we got on shore. He smiled and said, So Dick, the Work is done too quick; I had but just made an End of my Insurance. He applied to me to make Protest of the Loss of the Ship. About three Weeks or a Month after, the Prisoners were taken into Custody, upon James Bather's Information. Benson desired us all to swear to the Protest. I went over to Barnstaple, and when I returned, the Captain and Mate, and my Brother Sinnett, were taken in Custody. Benson said, if I did not swear to the Protest it would cost the Captain his Life.

Q. Was Lloyd one of those saved in the Boat?

Sinnett. He was; I believe he was concerned in launching the Boat. I was in Company with Powe in the Isle of Lundy before the Ship set out. When he proposed to me a Note for Money, I proposed to have 10 1. more, which was granted and added to the aforesaid Note, and writing on the back, but did not say at what Time it should be paid.

Cross-examined.

Q. How many Men were there on board?

Sinnett. There were three Sailors, besides the Captain, two Mates, two Boys and a Man Cook, besides 15 or 16 Transports.

Q. Was Lloyd acquainted with any of these Transactions?

Sinnett. I don't know that he was , only in making his Escape with the rest.

Council for the Crown. Was the Design of destroying the Ship made a Secret of on board?

Sinnett. I don't know whether all Hands knew it or not.

Q. from Lancey. Whether or no I knew of the Combustibles on board?

Sinnett. He bid me to go to such a Vessel and cut it abroad; and the Hole in the bulk-head was cut right against the Combustibles.

After Sinnett had completed his evidence, James Bather was called.

James Bather. I was shipped on board the *Nightingale*, 'Squire Benson Owner, about 20 Months ago, I was shipped by the Prisoner Powe. I had come home Passenger in one of Mr. Benson's Vessels, and owed Mr. Powe some Money, and when I saw him would have shunned him; he called me to him, and asked me to go with such a Vessel; I told him I had made a very bad Summer's Work of it, and could not pay him; he said, if you will go in the *Catherine* or *Nightingale*, you shall make your Summer's Work, your Year's Work double. I did not understand what he meant by that. He said, You shall go Boatswain of the *Nightingale*, and have 30s. a Month; I agreed to it, and went and helped rig the Vessel, and was on board when she sailed from Appledore to the Isle of Lundy, and anchored in that Road in 14 Fathom Water; after that Marshall and Magra came on board. Lancey and Powe were there; Powe said to me, Have you a Mind to accept a Note for 40 1. in case an Accident should happen in the Voyage outward bound? I Asked them in what Shape? Powe said, by way of Security for your Clothes and Chest. I refused it, but said 45 1. might do; accordingly it was wrote upon the Back of the Note, clear Money. I being ignorant, did not know how the Note was drawn, or when payable. I had it some Time, and afterwards it was sent to Lundy.

Q. Were your Clothes and Chest worth 45 1.?

Bather. No, nor 20 1. neither.

Q. Why was your Note sent to Lundy?

Bather. Because we were afraid of carrying them with us, for fear they should be burnt; for it had been talked of in the Cabin by Mr. Powe that the Ship should be destroyed. Lancey wrote the Notes, and Powe signed them. Lloyd was not there at that Time. I am not certain whether I received the Note from Lancey or Powe. The next Evening a Boat came from the Island; the Captain and Lloyd were then on board; Lancey himself hung up a Tarpaulin, that the Convicts might not see what Things were brought up; the Boat came once the first Night, and twice the second, and carried away 17 or 18 Bales of Cloth, and two large and four small Maunds; there remained 350 Bushels of Salt, with Mats about it, to keep it from the Sides of the Ship. We sailed from Lundy on Sunday Morning, and sailed all Day and all Night; on Monday Morning we saw a Vessel; she came up and spoke with us, sailed, and might be a League and a half from us, before the Captain ordered Richard Sinnett to go and cut a Hole in the Bulk-head. After Sinnett came up, and said he had cut himself, Lancey ordered me to go down and cut a hole betwixt the Bread-room and Salt, in order to put a Candle in. I went down and did it; and afterwards, by his Orders, bored a hole in the Ship's Bottom; I stopped it with a Marling-Spike, and went on Deck to see where the Philadelphia-man was. After the Boat was hoisted out, Lancey ordered me to go down and set fire to the Ship; accordingly I went down with a Candle into the Bread-room, and looked through; I saw Oakum dipped in Tar, drew some of it near me, and set fire to it; then I ran up upon Deck; the Captain was there: he called down to the Prisoners, and said, What are you about? What have you done? You have set fire to the Ship. They were greatly surprised, and said they knew nothing of it; the Captain said he was ruined, and desired to Boat to be hoisted out; we cleared the Prisoners, and went into the Boat, Convicts and all; two or three of us went on Pretence to put out the Fire, after it was gone too far. The Philadelphia-man came and took us in. Capt. Lancey gave Lloyd a blue Coat; I had a Coat, Waistcoat, and Shirt given me; we got safe on Shore, and in two or three Days after, saw Mr. Benson. He called us into the great Parlour, and gave each of us a Dram, and desired us to go and swear to the Protest; we said we would not unless he gave us fresh Notes.

Q. Did you swear to the Protest?

Bather. I did; and the next Day went to Exeter, to make a Discovery of it. I went to Mr. Code, an underwriter, and swore that the Protest was false.

Q. Have you received any money upon the Note?

Bather. I have received 5 l. 2s. of Mr. Powe, and he told me when the Insurance Money was recovered I should be paid the rest.

Anthony Metherall, second Mate, confirmed the several Particulars deposed to by the foregoing Witnesses, in relation to the Transactions at Lundy, and the boring and firing of the Ship; and added, that he heard Lloyd say, as they were going near Appledore, he was to have 60 l. for his Share, but did not say what for; that he told this to a Boy, because he had a Suspicion that the Boy had made a Discovery; so this was said to him to cause him to keep it secret.

Thomas Sharpe, a Cabin Boy in the same Ship, deposed to the same Effect.

Q. from Lancey. Did you see me concerned in any notes, or landing the Goods?

Sharpe. No I did not.

Francis Shackstone, a Mariner on board the *Nightingale*, gave evidence that when he came on board he had a Note delivered to him for 45 1. signed by Powe; the Purport of which Note was, that in case the Ship was lost, between that and the Cape Virginia, he, the Deponent, was to have so much Money. The rest of his Evidence entirely corresponded with what had been before given by the other Witnesses; except only with this Addition, that he received of Powe to the Amount of 45 1. on account of the Note after he came home.

Q. from Lancey. Was I by when the Note was given you by Mr. Powe.

Shackstone. Yes; this was in Bideford, at a Cook's Shop; when I was desired to sign the Protest, upon which a fresh Note was given me.

The Council for the Crown closed their Evidence by shewing the Policies, and called Mr. Edward Maund to prove one for 400 1. in the Names of Liddel, Toucher, Rook, and Biscoe, for each 100 1. This Policy was made out by Order of Mr. Benson, as Maund proved by a letter of Benson's own Handwriting.

Q. How much was insured on the Cargo of this Ship?

Maund. There was 800 1. at first, and 900 1. by a subsequent Order.

The Council for the Crown said they had other Policies to produce, to prove that the Ship and Cargo were insured for 2100 1. but this being sufficient to shew the Intention of the Defraud, they would rest it here.

The principal Objections that arose from Matter of Law, urged by the Council for the Prisoners, were in favour of Powe; thus:

1. Whether the Crime he was charged with, is within the Jurisdiction of the Admiralty of England? That of a Person, as an Accessory, upon Land, to the Burning of a Ship, and if that is committed afterwards on the High Seas, it was submitted to the Court, whether he was not liable to be indicted at the Assize for the County where the Offence was committed; and the Isle of Lundy was in the County of Devon.

2. That in the Statute upon which the Indictment was founded, the 11th of George I. Cap. 21. the Words are, as to this Crime, 'It is, amongst

other Things enacted, That if any Owners of, or Captain, Master, Mariner, or other Officer belonging to any Ship, should, after the 24th of June, which shall be in the Year of our Lord 1718, wilfully cast away, burn, or otherwise destroy the Ship of which he shall be Owner, or unto which she shall belong, or in any Manner of ways direct or procure the same to be done, to one, or of any Merchant or Merchants, that shall load Goods thereon, he shall suffer Death.' That this Clause does not run in general Words, but is confined to Persons either concerned as Owners or Mariners, and that Powe, being a Taylor by Trade, and lived at Appledore-point, in the County of Devon, and was neither Owner, Captain, Master or Mariner, it was submitted to the Court, whether he could be found guilty of the Crime he was charge with?

Capt. Lancey, in his Defence said, that at the Isle of Lundy he took in Provisions, but took nothing out of the Ship; that he sailed as soon as the Wind permitted ; that the Ship, contrary to his Knowledge, took fire, and had not the Boat been hoisted out immediately, all their lives would have been lost; after which they were taken up by Capt. Nicholson, and that each of these Witnesses signed the Protest.

Lloyd said, that whatever was acted on board the Ship, was a Secret to him; and he knew nothing of the Affair.

Powe said, he knew nothing of the Bills they charged him with, that he never gave them such Orders as they had said, and that the man who swore against him was in his Debt.

To Capt. Lancey's Character, Mr. Merryweather said, he had known Capt. Lancey ever since he came to Town; that he came to his House from the Gaol at Exeter, and might have gone away if he would; that the Jailor trusted him to go to the Play twice, and he had the Honour to return.

Daniel Nicholls said, he had known Capt. Lancey ever since he was a Child, and had sailed with him some Years, and that he is as Good and well-behaved a Man as ever he sailed with in his Life, and did not think he would be guilty of setting fire to his Ship ion order to cheat the Insurers.

Lancey. Please to call Capt. Marshall to my Character.

Marshall. I have known Capt. Lancey from a Child. He has had as good a Character as any Man in the World, before this Accident happened.

Several Persons appeared to the Characters of Powe and Lloyd, and spoke very handsomely of them; especially of the last, of whom it was said, that if there was an honest Man in the world, he was one.

The Evidence being closed for the Prisoners, the Council for the Prosecution replied to the Objections before mentioned by this Prisoner's Council, to this Purport.

To the first, that no Person can set fire to a Ship at Sea, that is not Master, Captain, or Mariner, and therefore such only can be considered as principal Felons; and it having come out, that the Master did set her on fire because he ordered it; and therefore he is indictable as a Principal on this Act of Parliament: If so, then any Person that instigates, incites, or advises the Mariners on board to commit the Fact, is an Accessory before the Felony committed, at Common-law, that being made do by the Stature, and therefore triable in this Court.

To the second, 'twas answered, if the Crime Powe was charged with, had been committed in the Body of the County of Devon, there would have been some Colour for that Objection; but the Notes were given by him in the Cabin of the Ship *Nightingale*, as she was riding at Anchor in the Road of Lundy, where the Tide has its Flux and Reflux; which is the same as if she had been ever so many Leagues from Shore, and is certainly triable in the Jurisdiction of the high court of Admiralty, for inciting, moving, instigating, stirring up, persuading, advising, &c.

The trial lasted for seven hours. The Jury retired to consider their verdict and found Lancey guilty, Lloyd not guilty, and in the case of Powe that "before the Said Felony was committed by Lancey, near the Isle of Lundy, he did incite, instigate, move, stir up and counsel the said Lancey to commit the same; but they found him neither Owner, Captain nor Mariner, and so referred it to the Judge".

The Judge pronounced sentence; Lancey "let him be hanged by the neck until he be dead"; Powe "let him remain until further order". Lloyd was acquitted. After his long ordeal, John Sinnett was delivered from prison by proclamation.

John Sinnett and Lloyd, free to return to their homes, are heard of no more.

James Bather cashed in on the sensation created throughout the country by the Old Bailey trial, by publishing a pamphlet, rather grandly titled, "A Full and Faithful Account of the Life of James Bather, late Boatswain of the *Nightingale*, Brig." – a testament of dubious value which attempted, with little success, to excuse his part in the affair.

Powe was brought up for trial at Exeter Assizes in March, 1754, charged with "compounding a Felony committed by Tho. Benson, Esq.," but, as Benson had fled the country, the case was held over till the following year and Powe was remanded. He was held in gaol until his final discharge in 1758.

Lancey was returned to Newgate Gaol to await his Execution. On May 30th, 1754, an Admiralty Order signed by the Admirals Anson, Duncannon, Ellis and Boscawen, directed Sir Thomas Salisbury, "that you convey the said John Lancey unto the Gallows set and placed in the public stream in the River Thames within the Flux of the sea and water and Jurisdiction of our Admiralty aforesaid, before the Bank called Wapping, on Friday, the seventh day of the month of June next, and him the said John Lancey at the time of the Reflux of the Sea and Water there you hang him by the neck until he be dead according to the Maritime Customs anciently used and observed."

Protesting his innocence until the last, he published his own account of the *Nightingale* affair, very much as convicted criminals do at the present time and, no doubt, with the same purpose to make some provision for their wives and families.

An account of Lancey's last few days in gaol is given by the Ordinary, or Chaplain of Newgate. The Ordinaries of Newgate were famous for attributing pious statements to the blackest of villains, and for recording fictitious last speeches of hanged criminals to convince the world that they died as penitent christians. His account, though it does the greatest credit to John Lancey, must, therefore, be treated with reserve; he records "In several conversations that passed between the Prisoner and me, I don't remember that he expressed any Resentment, against either his Prosecutors, or Bather who made the Discovery, whose Account he admitted, in general, to be true. For two Days and two Nights, he would not suffer his prayers to be interrupted, even by Sleep, and to his last Hour, behaved with a steadiness and composure, very seldom seen on the like Solemn Occasion".

On Friday, June 17th, 1754, Captain Lancey met his barbarous end. Hangings were the occasion for a public holiday, and all the town turned out to watch the fun, the apprentice boys, the pick-pockets and the gin sodden harlots, all determined to enjoy themselves. They took up their places the night before and passed the time drinking, dancing and copulating in the streets. The quality and, on occasions, even Royalty, watched from the upper windows of neighbouring houses, and celebrated the spectacle with lavish champagne breakfasts. There was a carefully observed ritual on these occasions. The chaplain pronounced prayers for the condemned man who usually made a last speech to the crowd. The execution itself was a protracted business. As the drop was not long enough to break the neck of the condemned man, his dangling body performed a convulsive dance in mid-air to the vast amusement of the crowd. And so Lancey died at Wapping, where Captain Kidd and other notorious pirates had been hanged before him.

The account of his hanging in the "Gentleman's Magazine" says, almost superfluously, "Captain Lancey was hanged at Execution Dock and behaved very penitently".

CHAPTER X

EXILE

Benson's prospects of a life of exile in Portugal were bleak indeed. There seemed little to hope for in the dreary years that lay ahead. Utter ruination faced him with his fortune gone and his estates and the family home at Knapp seized by the Sheriff of Devon, whose high office he had once held. The death of his wife deprived him of her companionship when most he needed it and spelt a life of loneliness. There was, however, one small source of consolation to relieve the gloomy prospect and which, perhaps, he had foreseen when he had made over his trading vessels to the Melhuishes.

They had given instructions to the master of the *Peter* and the *Placentia* to proceed from Newfoundland to Lisbon in order, curious as it might seem, for them to sell their vessels there. This proved to be a most convenient arrangement for Benson. The vessels arrived at Oporto on the 11th December, safely beyond the jurisdiction of the Court of Exchequer, and the masters were there to greet him when he landed later that month. Benson celebrated his first Christmas day in Portugal by dining the two captains. One can imagine him relaxed in their company, after the constant anxiety and the humiliations of the last twelve months, recovering much of his former buoyant spirits and, viewing the world more rosily as they drank to the future in excellent port wine, confiding to them his plans for making a bigger fortune than ever.

Two months later, sometime in February 1754, Thomas Higg, master of the *Peter*, sold this vessel to Jose Antonio Lima for 500 moidores. there is no record of what happened to the *Placentia*. It seems more than probable that Benson kept the vessel and with the 500 moidores as capital, embarked on his new career as a merchant trading from Oporto. By a strange caprice of fate, Benson's fortunes began to look more hopeful at the very time that Lancey faced his trial at the Old Bailey.

Benson was kept in touch with events at home, by regular correspondence from his lawyer, Narcissus Hatherly, from his trustees, and from his nephew, young Thomas Stafford. The news that they gave him was uniformally grim. Though he must have foreseen the outcome of the Old Bailey Trial, the news of Lancey's death sentence came as a shock and filled him with remorse, which was to haunt him until the end of his days. The thought that Lancey's staunch, unquestioning loyalty had saved his life troubled his mind and gave him no peace. He wrote to his son Peter, requesting him to provide Lancey's wife with a small regular income. He wrote this, no doubt, in an effort to ease his conscience, although he must have been aware from the recent reports from Narcissus Hatherly that it would be almost impossible for Peter to carry out the request. Hatherly had informed him that the Sheriff of Devon, on orders from the Court of Exchequer, had sold up his effects and much of his property, to pay off part of Benson's debt to the Crown. Knapp and the remainder of the family estate, were to be held by the Sheriff until the trustees had paid the debt in full. The old lawyer had other news too, which gave him cause for grave concern.

The circumstances of the trial had created a sensation throughout the country and aroused a great deal of sympathy for Lancey. There was a widespread demand that Benson should be brought back to England to face his trial, which found expression in the popular press ... "The virtue, however, which so long prevented his (Lancey's) concurrence with Benson, now prevented his divulging the secret with which he had been entrusted, though he was offered not only his life, but his liberty, upon that condition. However, after he had thus refused to preserve himself by giving up Benson, he had heard that Benson had deserted him, though he continued to abuse his confidence by repeated assurances of protection, by his influence and his wealth, till the very hour in which he secretly left the kingdom.

"To punish such an offender uncommon diligence should be exerted; and it is surely to be wished that our resident in the kingdom where he had taken shelter, should be instructed to demand, that he should be given up as an enemy, not to one country only, but to the world, as a pest of society and a disgrace to mankind."

The Government appeared to have made an application for Benson's extradition and in June 1754, the "Gentleman's Magazine" reported, "It is said that Mr. Benson was obliged to shift his place of exile at Oporto on account of very strong influences made at the Portuguese court for delivering him up." Forewarned of these moves, Benson had slipped away some seventy miles north, safely across the Spanish border, and made his new home in Vigo.

Here he received news of Lancey's grim end at Execution Dock and was, perhaps, to endure the most terrible days of his life, days and nights haunted by regret and remorse.

The time passed heavily. Trading in a small way with the *Placentia*, his only vessel, yielded meagre returns, and contrasted pitifully with his former flourishing enterprises. He had time to reflect that at home, his rival merchants of Barnstaple and Bideford, led, no doubt, by the public spirited Matthew Reeder, were grabbing for themselves whatever they could of the vast trade which he had built up.

At home, too, the last act in the tangled affairs of his family estates dragged on endlessly through the Court of Exchequer, a dreary anti-climax. That year his sister, Catherine Stafford, brought before the Court a case suing Benson and the Attorney General. Her object was to salvage from the family estates, still held by the Sheriff, the legacies left to her children by their uncle Peter, which had been left on trust to Benson until such time as they either married or attained the age of twenty-one. Four years later his affairs once more occupied the attention of the Court. A certain Edward Maunde, who claimed to be a creditor of Benson's, sued him through his trustees and Narcissus Hatherly for the recovery of the debt. Captain Hogg's evidence in this case brought to light the movements of the *Peter* and the *Placentia*, and, during the hearing, John Underwood gave evidence of Benson being hounded by his creditors during his stay in London. As a result of this case, Benson was adjudged to be bankrupt.

By this time England was once more at war with France, a war that was being fought out by Clive in India, by Wolfe in Canada, and by Boscawen and Hawke upon the high seas. The whole of the energies of the Government, now led by Pitt, were bent on defeating France. Every day brought momentous news for the English public, the execution of Admiral Byng, the horror of the Black Hole of Calcutta, Admiral Hawke's victory at Quiberon, and Wolfe's storming the heights of Quebec.

With so much of importance to occupy the minds of all at home, Benson may well have felt that he was now forgotten and that it would be safe for him to make a quiet return to Oporto. Here he was joined in exile by his favourite nephew, Thomas Stafford. This act of faith by one of his family, did much to rekindle his old spirit of adventure, his determination and his restless energy. There had always been a close bond of affection between them, much closer than existed between Benson and his own children, and the two men set out to rebuild the family estate. Benson had many old friends among the Portuguese merchants, who now proved ready to help him at this time when his fortunes were at their lowest ebb. Within a few years, this very remarkable man, assisted by his nephew, had built up one of the greatest English trading companies in Portugal. Perhaps in the ceaseless work which this entailed, he found some escape from the bitter memories of the past, from the thoughts of Lancey's execution which haunted his mind, and from the almost physical longing to see his native Devon once more.

It is fascinating to probe the motives that impelled Benson to take such a rash step as the destruction of the *Nightingale*, and difficult to understand why a man of his wealth and position should have hazarded all his career by such an action. It was no sudden impulse, for the whole episode was carefully planned at every stage. As he was a wealthy man at the time, no urgent financial necessity explains the reason. Possibly the views he expressed on the shipping of convicts to Lundy provide some clue. Benson did not regard this as fraudulent in any way, but rather as an act of good business. As he saw it, the Government were merely concerned to have the convicts transported out of England, and for his part it was much more profitable to take them to Lundy, rather than to have the expense of a long voyage across the Atlantic to the Colonies. Probably Benson took a similar view of the *Nightingale*, considering it was just good business to dispose of the old brigantine in the most profitable way. In his view there were no moral considerations involved. The accepted morals of the Eighteenth Century, a period of great corruption and robustness of outlook, were vastly different from those of our present highly regulated age, and Benson was very much a man of his period.

Had his plan not miscarried, Thomas Benson may well have been regarded as one of the great worthies of Devon, instead of his name going down to history as a notorious villain. His despicable act in leaving Lancey to pay with his life, for a crime of which he himself was the author, is difficult to excuse and it earned him the hatred of his fellow men. The scandal of this act has lived on long after men have forgotten his achievements, the part he played in fostering the prosperity of the thriving ports of Appledore and Bideford, providing most of the population of these towns with their livelihood, and doing more for the cultivation and improvement of Lundy than any previous owner or tenant of the Island.

Death came to him peacefully in Oporto at the age of sixty four, and with him there passed away, perhaps for ever, that spirit of buccaneering born in Devon with Raleigh, Hawkins, Drake and Grenville.

By a strange quirk of fate, his death foreshadowed the end of an era in the history of the ports of Appledore and Bideford, which owed so much of their prosperity to his enterprise. Ever since the days of Grenville, Bideford had thrived upon the trade with the American Colonies, but within a year or two of Benson's death the colonies revolted against the government of George III, and, aided by France and Spain, gained their independence. The trade with America never returned to these ports; it was the end of a long era of prosperity.

Much has changed in the life of North Devon since Benson's time. Barnstaple and Bideford have ceased to be ports of any consequence. no longer do the fishing fleets, some fifty strong, sail from Bideford across the Atlantic, bound for the Newfoundland fisheries. Gone is the ceaseless flow of shipping, carrying locally made woollen goods to Portugal, Spain and America; gone too is the woollen industry itself, for centuries the main source of prosperity to North Devon. Little now remains of the great maritime trade that Benson did so much to foster.

But the granite walls of Lundy still stand as his fitting memorial.

BIBLIOGRAPHY

My main sources have been "A Genuine Account of the Burning of the *Nightingale*, Brig" by John Lancey (London 1754), "A Full and Faithfull Account of the Life etc." by James Bather (London 1755), the "Gentleman's Magazine", and various unpublished documents in the Public Record Office. For the historical background I am indebted to "The Whig Supremacy" by Basil Williams, "England in the Eighteenth Century" by J.H. Plumb and "Devon" by W. G. Hoskins.

Lundy has a surprisingly large literature of its own and some of the books that refer to Benson are:

Chater, J.R.	Lundy Island	(London 1877)
Etherton, P.T. & Barlow, V.	Tempestuous Isle	(London 1950)
Lloyd, L.R.W.	Lundy, its history and natural history	(London 1925)
Page, J. de W.	The coasts of Devon and Lundy Island	(London 1895)

Benson has been portrayed as the villain in two works of fiction; "Captain Stauncey's Vow", which was serialised in "The Leisure Hour" of 1862, a florid Victorian melodrama which, though historically inaccurate, makes amusing reading; and "Ivor" by George Russell (London 1911), a light romantic novel, which is a purely imaginative story.

DETAILED REFERENCES

CHAPTER I

Much of the family history is derived from the Exchequer Records, P.R.O. (Reference Number E134/33 Geo.II/Mich.).

Information on the Tobacco Trade of Bideford and the Fisheries is taken from the "Universal Magazine" of 1749 and from "Ships and Shipyards of Bideford" by Inkerman Rogers.

The facts about the "Benson Galley" are taken from the "Gentleman's Magazine", 1744, pages 423, 535 and 592.

Details of the election of 1747 are drawn from an article by Viscount Ebrington in the "Nineteenth Century" of June 1889.

CHAPTER II

The case of the *Grace* is to be found in the Public Record Office (Reference E159/598 25/Geo.II/Mich.II).

The description of the visit to Lundy comes from "The North Devon Magazine" published in Barnstaple 1824.

CHAPTER III

The main details are taken from "A Genuine Account of the Burning of the *Nightingale*, Brig" and "A Full and Faithful Account of the Life of James Bather".

Details of the Bill of Lading may be found in the Public Record Office under reference TI/352.

CHAPTERS IV, V & VI

All the facts are taken from Lancey's and Bather's accounts of the *Nightingale* affair, and from the account of Lancey's trial published in "Select Trials at the Sessions-House in the Old Bailey". Vol.III.(London, 1764).

CHAPTER VII

I have drawn on the "History of Newgate and the Old Bailey" by W. Eden Hooper and "The Old Bailey and Newgate" by Charles Gordon (London, 1903) for much information in this chapter.

John Sinnett's letters are taken from "A Genuine Account, etc." by John Lancey.

CHAPTER VIII

All the information in this chapter is taken from the Public Record Office. The cases of *Britannia* and *Nightingale* may be found under the references E159/599 Trinity Term 25/26 Geo.II. Devon 5 and 8, and E159/599 Easter Term 26 Geo.II. Middx. 4, 7, 8, 9, 10, 11, 12, 13 and 14.

For details of Benson's visit to London and his instructions to the master of the *Peter*, see reference E134/32 Geo.II/Mich.

The details of the information in the case of the *Ropeyard* may be found under reference HCA.1.58/

The correspondence between the Commissioners of the Customs and the Treasury is under reference T1/352.

Benson's Memorial regarding his estates is under reference T1/354.

CHAPTER IX

The account of the trial is taken from 'Select Trials at the Sessions-House in the Old Bailey", Vol.III.(London, 1764).

CHAPTER X

The demand for Benson to be brought back to England is quoted from the "Gentleman's Magazine", June 1754, page 279.

The two cases brought before the Court of Exchequer by Catherine Stafford and Edward Maude may be found in the Public Record Office under references E134/33 Geo.II/Mich. and E134/32 Geo.II/Mich.

SOME ADDITIONAL NOTES

p 13. Grenado: shot fired from a mortar piece. It could be incendiary.

pp 14, 18, 19, 58. I have found no evidence for any close connection between Benson and the Lords Gower and Carteret. Lundy was a very minor part of their large landholdings, which were administered by agents. Gower and Carteret took very little, if any, interest in their estates in Devon and Cornwall.

Ref: Duke of Sutherland's papers held by Staffordshire Record Office, and Chancery proceedings from 1762, Public Record Office.

p 14. After the punch bowl was given to Barnstaple Corporation, it was politely pointed out that they had no ladle. Benson provided one, engraved with "He that gave the bowl gave the ladle."

pp 15, 16. In order to convert 1740-1750 moneys to 1999 values, the figures should be multiplied by 78.67. The £4000 spent on the election thus represents £314,680, or just over £974 per head of the electorate. Benson's fine of £8229 (p.59) represents £647,375.

p 19. Rowse, 1937, states that Richard Grenville acquired Lundy c.1577 from his father-in-law, Sir John St Leger, in settlement of a debt.

In 1751 Lundy was the joint possession in equal shares of John Leveson Gower, Earl Gower, and John Carteret, Earl Granville. In that year Gower took a lease of Carteret's moiety [half] for 21 years at a rent of £30 per annum, as from June 24th. On July 2nd 1751 Gower granted a lease of the whole island to Thomas Benson for 21 years, at a rent of £60 per annum, also dated from June 24th. The lease provided for Benson to buy the island for £1500 but he did not do this, which suggests that he may already have been short of liquid capital. The terms of the lease also stated that if the rent remained unpaid for 14 days of the due date, or the demand, then Gower would be entitled to re-possess the island.

Thomas states that Benson rented Lundy from 1748, which is probably taken from Chanter, 1871. If this were so, then the lease of 1751 would have been a renewal made necessary by the transfer of Carteret's moiety to Gower. On present information it is not possible to resolve this question.

p 20. In the circumstances, no-one would have reported the escape of the convicts, which enabled them to get clear away.

p 21. There would have been a minimal economical factor in taking the convicts to Lundy rather than to America, since Benson's ships were trading there in any case. Their value lay in the transportation fees, and in providing slave labour for work on Lundy, which at that time stood much in need of improvement.

The wall referred to as built by Benson I now think to have been Quarter Wall. Early references, before the Heaven ownership, refer to the land lying beyond Quarter Wall as the north, or the uncultivated part of the island.

p 28. There were 15 convicts; this equates with the transportation fee of £60, which was £5 per head (Morgan, 1992). Benson's contracts, and the names of the convicts are found in North Devon Record Office, and date from 1746 to 1752. Pp 30, 35, 39, 43 point to Bather's having been a very unreliable witness. The transportation bond was made between Benson and Robert Incledon, Clerk of the Peace, Devon, not with the Government. The terms provided for the convicts to be taken from Exeter gaol "to some of his Majesty's colonies and Plantations in America." Benson was obliged to deliver a bond (in 1752 for £60) which could be recovered only against the receipt for the delivery of the prisoners at their destination. Also, a fine of £30 would be levied if the contract were not carried out within three months.

There is no record of how many convicts were held on Lundy, but as the journalist of 1752 and Bather stated that there were only three houses, "one large [occupied by the convicts] and two small," and some prisoners had stolen a boat and escaped, it probably was not a great number. Benson would have stood to lose his bond money if the prisoners were not delivered in America, and there are two possibilities whereby he may have avoided this. Either he worked hand-in-glove with corrupt officials and forged papers (which at that time was quite likely). Or he may have landed one or two useful convicts from each transport who, when the ship arrived in America, would be declared to have died on the voyage and been buried at sea.

p 30. "Returned to Lundy," i.e. went ashore from the ship anchored in the Bay.

p 33. The cave, which has been been excavated and is not a natural cavern, has long been referred to as Benson's Cave, on no more than an assumption that Benson used it for smuggled goods. However, the graffiti found on the interior walls date from 1726, so the construction pre-dates Benson's tenancy. The statements of the crew at the trial make it clear that Benson's goods were buried and not hidden in the cave. Although the cave is well concealed and not visible to anyone unaware of its existence, Richard Scores was found by Customs men to have been smuggling on Lundy c.1721. Therefore it is likely that these previous searches by the Customs would have rendered the cave useless for concealment afterwards.

p 40. 130 1 = £130

p 42. Only by a consolidated agreement to stick to their story was there any hope for Benson and the ship's crew to escape conviction for insurance fraud, since the necessary evidence to back Bather's story would be withheld. Unfortunately for them, the agreement did not include Marshall, and once Benson had fled and the situation was so threatening, the remainder of the crew spoke out to save themselves.

p 46. Maund: basket. Poultry Compter: the prison at the Poultry, London.

p 65. Clarke: clerk in holy orders.

p 67, 68. Brickbat: piece of brick, usually used as a missile. Possibly, in this case, used as ballast.

p 81, 82. The writer of 1752 later added to his journal that after 15 or 16 years Benson returned to his house at "Napp [his wife]" where he stayed incognito for 5 or 6 months before returning to Portugal. He was also said to have returned again a few years later, when he stayed for a year or more. These reports may well have rested on rumour, especially as Thomas records that Benson's wife died in January of 1753 (p 59). A further complication is that Drake wrote in 1941 that Benson's wife re-married twice after his death (1772), and gives a Mr John Benson as his authority. Either Benson married for a second time, or the death of his first wife was mis-reported. It seems unlikely that a figure so well known in North Devon could have returned, and remained, incognito, and that he would have done so at the risk of imprisonment for debt.

p 82. Benson's wealth in 1752 was questionable, since he was unable to pay his creditors (p57), his fines, or to find money for the crew's bail. It is also in question whether he hazarded his all on the *Nightingale*, or whether this was the occasion when he was found out. The story of the *Snow*, or *Ropeyard* (p58), suggests that the *Nightingale* may not have been the first operation of this kind.

BENSON'S SHIPS:

When his father died in 1739 Benson inherited "property at Appledore, a number of merchantmen and £1000. His elder brother, Peter, died in 1743, unmarried, and Benson inherited his assets, which included ships, and lime and ash works.

Catherine, Grace, Dolphin, Newkay, Nightingale, Peter, Placentia.

Taken by the enemy in 1744: *Benson Galley, Britannia, Mont, Prosperous, Vine.*

Taken by the enemy in 1745: *Resolution.*

BIBLIOGRAPHY

Anon, "Benson, MP and Smuggler," *The Hartland Chronicle*, 1906.

Bank of England Information Office, "Equivalent values of the Pound: 1270-1999."

Chanter, J.R., 1871, "A History of Lundy Island," *Transactions of the Devonshire Assn*, iv, pp 553-603.

Devon Record Office, Q/S 129/21-40 (1741-60).

Drake, D., 1941, "Members of Parliament for Barnstaple 1689-1832," *Transactions of the Devonshire Assn.*, lxxiii, p. 185.

The Gentleman's Magazine, 1754, xxiv, pp 176-77, 244, 278-79.

Jamieson, A., 1992, "Devon & Smuggling 1680-1850," Duffy *et al*, Eds, *"The New Maritime History of Devon,"* i.

Morgan, K., 1992, 'Convict Transportation from Devon to America,' Duffy *et al*, Eds, *"The New Maritime History of Devon,"* i.

The North Devon Magazine, 1824. (Journals of 1752, 1787).

North Devon Record Office, B 1114/30: Thomas, S., research notes.

Porter, R: 1982, *English Society in the Eighteenth Century*.

Public Record Office, B 114/30; HCA 1/58; T 1/352.

Chancery proceedings, 1762-1779, The Dowager Lady Gower v Granville, Earl Gower.

Romney & Sedgewick, Eds., *The History of Parliament: the House of Commons*, i, pp 454-56.

Rowse, A.L., 1937, *Sir Richard Grenville of the Revenge*.

Smith, G., 1980, *Something to Declare*.

Stafford Record Office, D/593/C/21/4/1.

Ternstrom, M., 1998, "The Ownership of Lundy by Sir Richard Grenville and his Descendants, 1577-1775," *Transactions of the Devonshire Association*, cxxx, pp. 65-80.

Ternstrom, M., 1999, Unpublished PhD thesis: "Lundy: an analysis and comparative study of factors affecting the development of the island from 1577 to 1969, with a gazetteer of sites and monuments." ii vols, Cheltenham & Gloucester College of Higher Education.

Thomas, S., 1954, "Lundy Privateers," *Devon County Journal*, iv, pp 3, 12-13.

Myrtle Ternstrom, March 2001

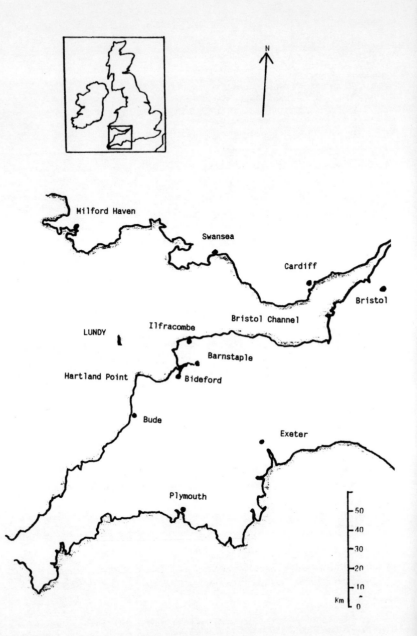

Map of Bristol Channel

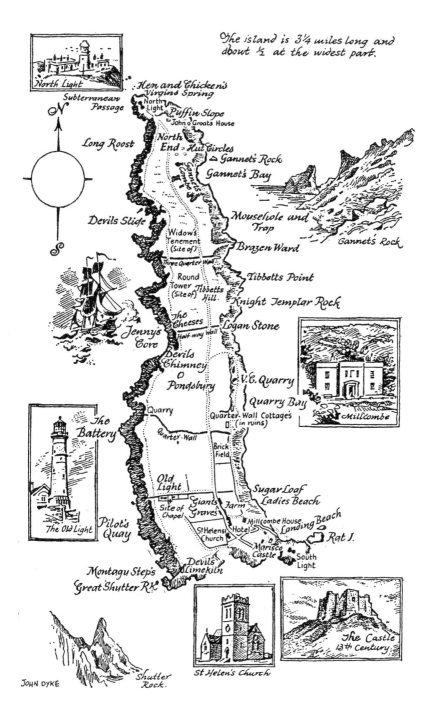

The island is 3¼ miles long and about ½ at the widest part.

North Light
Subterranean Passage

N
S

Hen and Chicken's
Virgins Spring
North Light
Puffin Slope
John o'Groat's House

Long Roost

North End
Hut Circles
Gannet's Rock
Gannet's Bay

Gannet's Combe

Devils Slide

Mousehole and Trap
Gannet's Rock

Widow's Tenement (Site of)
Brazen Ward

Three Quarter Wall

Round Tower (Site of)
Tibbetts Hill
Tibbetts Point
Knight Templar Rock

The Cheeses
Logan Stone

Jenny's Cove

Half-way Wall

Devils Chimney
Pondsbury

V.C. Quarry
Quarry Bay

The Battery

Quarry

Quarter Wall Cottages (in ruins)

Quarter Wall

Brick Field

Old Light

The Old Light

Pilot's Quay

Site of Chapel
Giants Graves
Farm

Sugar Loaf
Ladies Beach

St Helens Church
Hotel
Millcombe House
Landing Beach
Rat I.

Marisco Castle
South Light

Montagu Steps
Great Shutter Rk.

Devils Limekiln

Shutter Rock.

JOHN DYKE

Millcombe

St Helen's Church

The Castle
13th Century.

Map of Lundy, by kind permission of John Dyke